UPHOLSTERY

UPHOLSTERY

DOROTHY GATES

WARD LOCK LIMITED · LONDON

First published in Great Britain in 1986
by Ward Lock Limited, 8 Clifford Street, Mayfair,
London W1X 1RB, an Egmont Company.

Designed by Niki fforde
Drawings by Pam Corfield, advised by Dorothy Gates
Photography by Tom Mannion
Phototypeset in Bodoni by
Tradespools Limited, Frome, Somerset

Printed and bound in Italy by
Sagdos SpA

British Library Cataloguing in Publication Data

Gates, Dorothy
Upholstery.
1. Upholstery
I. Title
645'.4   TT198
ISBN 0-7063-6363-9

ACKNOWLEDGMENTS

Thanks to
Gatestone Upholstery of Carshalton, Surrey
for supplying furniture; Parker Knoll Textiles Ltd
High Wycombe, Bucks for supplying fabric (p43);
Michael Boys Syndication
for the photographs on page 27, 35 and 58.

Dedication

To My Dear Dad
(E.F. Stone F.A.M.U. A Master Upholsterer)
With love and thanks for teaching your children and
grandchildren the craft of upholstery.

CONTENTS

PART I UPHOLSTERY AND RE-UPHOLSTERY

1 Tools and equipment 7
2 Drop in seat 9
3 Stools and loose seats 13
4 Overstuff dining chair with sprung seat 15
5 Re-seating an easy chair 26
6 Easy chair with sprung back, sprung arms and independent sprung front edge 28
7 Wings and facings 36
8 Constructing a deep-button-backed headboard 37
9 Deep-button-backed, iron-frame chair 39

PART II COVERING AND RE-COVERING

10 Types of fabric for covering 44
11 Measuring and estimating 45
12 Piping and ruching 48
13 Sprung easy chair 50
14 Wings 59
15 Cushions 60
16 Headboards 65
17 Deep-button-backed chair 70
18 Trimmings and finishes 73
Useful Addresses 76
Glossary 77
Index 79

PART I
UPHOLSTERY AND RE-UPHOLSTERY

1 TOOLS AND EQUIPMENT

The following list gives a guide to the tools and equipment used during modern and traditional upholstery. A complete set of tools would be acquired over a long period.

Pair of tressles with a trough top, *or* a low table at least 1 m (1 yd) square
Sewing machine, with running foot and piping foot
Machine needles 14 to 18
Hammers: magnetic, cabriole and either two-headed or claw
Ripping chisel
Mallet
Web stretcher
Pincers
Bradawl
Scissors: blunt-end pair and one pair with 18 cm (7 in) blade
Steel rule
Metre stick
Tacks 16 mm (⅝ in), improved 13 mm (½ in) and fine 10 mm (⅜ in)
Gimp pins (assorted colours)
Mattress needles: assorted lengths, round and bayonet points
Spring needle, regulator, skewers

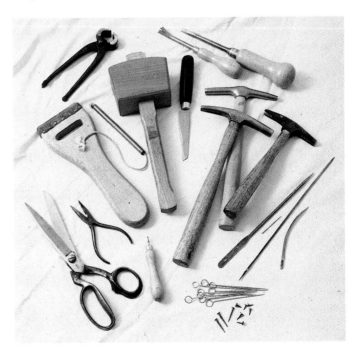

Some essential upholstery tools

Circular and cording needles
Knife
Staple gun and staples
Adhesive
Tack lifter

7

MATERIALS USED IN TRADITIONAL UPHOLSTERY

Algerian fibre: black in colour, is very similar to coir and has the same uses, but is more resilient.

Coir: fibre made from coconut husk, ginger in colour. It is used as a first stuffing.

Calico: a cotton fabric, made in different weights. It is used as an undercovering. A heavy calico is very strong and can be used as a top cover under loose covers.

Flock: made of cotton and waste fabrics. It can be milled and re-used as a filling but it is inclined to go 'lumpy' in use.

Hessian: a loosely-woven cloth made from jute. It is used as the main foundation in upholstery and comes in different densities. 283 g (10 oz) or 340 g (12 oz) are among the highest densities used.

Hair: usually horse hair, as this type is longer and keeps its curl (although it is not always available now). It is used as a top stuffing. It is very resilient and can be milled and re-used if in good condition. Hog's hair is sometimes used, but it is a much shorter hair and therefore lacks the qualities of horse hair.

Linette: black, fine-woven cloth used on the underside of chairs or loose seats. It is rather thin and does not stand up to a great deal of wear.

Piping cord: made from cotton strands, twisted into a cord and made in several thicknesses. It is used to make the piping (or welting) on the seams of furniture.

Scrim: a type of hessian weave made from the linen thread and therefore finer than hessian. It is used to cover the first stuffing on a seat, and when it has been stitched through, it forms a very strong stitched-up edge.

Springs: many types and sizes of spring are available. The double cone (or waisted spring) is the most commonly used; serpentine or wiggle springs are also in use. Rubber webbing can be used as a flat spring particularly on modern furniture.

Laid cord (lay cord): a thick cord used for lashing down the springs.

Linter felt: made from cotton lintas, this is a thick, soft padding used over the hair to prevent it penetrating through the outer cover. It is also used as an extra padding layer.

Threads and twine: linen thread is the strongest type. It is made in different thicknesses. Always use the best available. Twines are made from both linen and jute and can be waxed for easier handling.

Tarpaulin: a type of hessian weave that is very much heavier than ordinary hessian. It is sometimes called spring canvas and is used to cover over the springs.

Webbing: several types are available. The strongest and most expensive is the English type of webbing which is a black and white, herring-bone, linen weave. It is usually 5 cm (2 in) wide, but is also available in other widths. The other type of webbing used is made of jute, and is fawn in colour. It is very strong and available in different widths, 5 cm (2 in) being the most popular. Alternatively, polypropylene webbing is now available. It looks similar to the English webbing except that it is shiny. It is not as strong as the other types and is inclined to shred.

Wadding: sold by the metre (or yard), wadding looks like cotton wool enclosed in a thin skin. It comes in different weights and is used under the top cover to prevent wear on the fabric and to prevent hair from working its way through the top cover. Use the best one available as it is more economical to use one layer of a heavy wadding than two layers of a thin one.

MATERIALS USED IN MODERN UPHOLSTERY

Some of the materials in modern upholstery are identical to those used in traditional upholstery. In addition, however, the following materials are required.

Foam: latex foam is made from rubber which is

liquidized and poured into moulds in which air bubbles are allowed to form. It is made in different densities and types according to its function. The two types are pinhole and cavity: the pinhole is solid with air bubbles set at intervals and the cavity has a box-like construction on the inside and a moulded outer edge.

Plastic foam is made from polyether. It is made in many densities and is much lighter than rubber as well as being cheaper. It looks like a fine honeycomb and can be cut to size with a sharp knife.

Rubberized hair: made in sheets, it consists of hair covered in latex. It is usually sold approximately 5 cm (2 in) thick and can be cut to size as required.

Rubber webbing: very strong and used as a flat spring. It is sold in 5 cm (2 in) and 2.5 cm (1 in) widths.

Tension spring: a tightly wound spiral of wire covered with either a plastic or a fabric sleeve. It hooks on to either side of the frame. A row of tension springs make a spring seat or back.

Polyester or terylene wadding: similar in appearance to cotton wool. The wadding is used to wrap round cushions, to provide padding on backs and seats. Polyester wadding has a centre core and is usually thicker than terylene wadding.

Adhesives: several types are available. Each has a specific use for a particular material.

2 DROP IN SEAT

The traditional method of upholstery, or re-upholstery, requires a fair amount of skill and patience, as well as a good many years practise. It is much better to acquire the basic skills on a small item. One of the best pieces of furniture on which to practise is an overstuff seat, particularly if it is sprung. This type of chair incorporates nearly all the processes used in upholstery. A good alternative for the beginner is a drop-in dining seat which we will start on here. The first stage in re-upholstering is known as ripping out.

RIPPING OUT

Before beginning to re-upholster, the top cover and stuffings have to be removed. To do this, start at the underside of the seat and remove the bottom canvas using a ripping chisel and mallet. Insert the chisel under the head of a tack, and tap gently with the mallet until the tack starts to loosen. Exert downward pressure on the chisel, and give a hard tap on the end with the mallet;

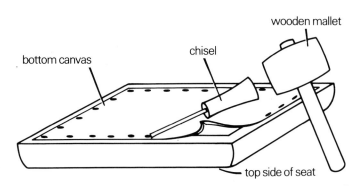

1 Ripping out a chair seat

the tack should come out clean. Always work along the grain of the wood in order not to split the frame. Before removing all the tacks, check the webbing and stuffing; sometimes a repair is all that is needed.

REMOVING BOTTOM CANVAS (HESSIAN OR LINETTE)

If the webbing and stuffing are in bad repair and need to be renewed, proceed with the removal of all the tacks. Remove the bottom canvas, the stuffing and the old webbing, making sure that no tacks are left in the frame. Check the joints for soundness and re-glue them at this stage if necessary.

WEBBING A SEAT

Using either English webbing (black and white) or a good quality jute webbing, proceed to web the seat in the following manner. Space the strips of webbing approximately 5 cm (2 in) apart, depending on the size of the seat. Do not skimp on the webbing, as this forms the main foundation for the seat. Place the first piece of webbing in position in the middle of the rail, and fold the raw end towards the centre of the seat. Place three 16 mm (5/8 in) improved tacks along the outer edge of the rail and hammer home. Place two more tacks towards the inner edge making a 'W' formation. This prevents the wood from splitting. If the rail is narrow or frail use a smaller tack 13 mm (1/2 in) fine.

Having fixed the webbing on one side, pull it towards the opposite side. Make a loop in the webbing, and thread it through the web stretcher. Use the web stretcher as a lever to pull the webbing until it is 'drum tight'. With three tacks fix the webbing onto this rail as before; cut the webbing, allowing enough to turn back. Turn back the end and tack down with two tacks in a 'W' formation. Continue to web the seat between the front and back rails. If the seat is wider across the front than the back, graduate the webbing to follow the frame line. When the webbing has been completed in one direction, weave the webbing, basket-fashion, from side to side and secure at each rail in the same manner as before.

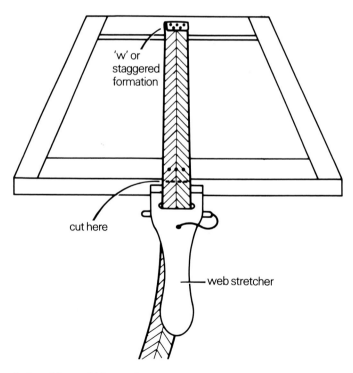

3 Attaching webbing to frame

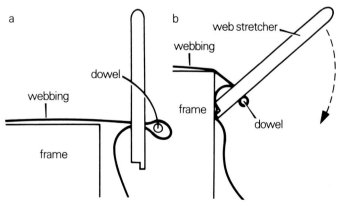

2 Using a web stretcher

10

4 Weaving the webbing

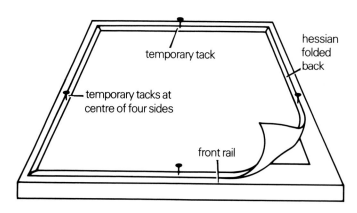

5 Applying the hessian

When the webbing has been completed, cut a length of hessian to fit the frame plus an allowance of 2.5 cm (1 in) all round to turn up. The hessian must be cut to the thread; this ensures that when it is turned over and tacked to the thread, it lies square. To apply the hessian, fold over a hem of 2.5 cm (1 in) on the front edge and place it along the front rail, so that it just covers the webbing. Place a temporary tack in the centre. (A temporary tack is one that is not tacked right home; it is a means of holding the fabric in place, and can easily be taken out and moved.)

Place a temporary tack in the centre back, centre front and centre sides. Working from the centre front, temporary tack out towards the corners, keeping the threads in the hessian straight along the front. Then repeat along the back and sides, again keeping the threads parallel to the sides. Keep the hessian taut while you tack. When you have tacked out from the four central points, work into the corners. Turn the corners over neatly and tack down. Hammer home all the tacks when satisfied that the hessian is square on the frame. The next stage is to apply bridle stitching to the hessian in order to secure the stuffing to the seat.

BRIDLE STITCHING

Bridle stitching is worked in rows across the seat using a spring needle and twine. A row of stitching every 10 cm (4 in) is about average, but the distance depends on the size of area to be covered. Use a good quality medium twine.

STUFFING

Using a good quality fibre, or hair if available, tease out the stuffing a handful at a time and push it under the

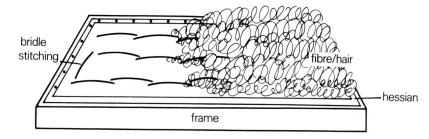

6 Section showing bridle stitching and stuffing

bridle stitching. Start at the back and work across the seat, gradually moving forwards until the whole seat is covered. Each time a handful of stuffing is added, tease it together with the stuffing around it until it all mats together. The objective is to achieve a smooth pad of evenly-distributed fibre. Add extra fibre to the centre of the seat in order to obtain a convex shape. The centre of the seat takes the most weight, and tends to flatten out or, worse still, form a hollow, if extra stuffing is not added at this stage.

COVERING WITH CALICO

After completing the stuffing, lay a piece of calico over the fibre. If the fibre or hair is very short or coarse, it may penetrate the calico. To prevent this, lay a thin layer of wadding between the fibre and the calico. The piece of calico should be long enough to cover the stuffing and the back edge of the frame.

Place a temporary tack in the centre of the back rail about 1.5 cm (⅝ in) from the lower edge. Do not turn the edge under, just leave it raw. (A fold would leave an impression that might show through the finished cover.)

Drop in seat with frame

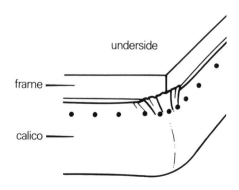

7 Fitting calico round the corner

Pull the calico forward and tack to the centre of the front rail, repeat this from side to side. Working out towards each corner, pull the calico with the left hand and push it with the right hand to give the maximum stretch; temporary tack in place.

When you reach the corners, pull from the centre of a corner, until the calico is stretched clean over the edge of the frame. Tack home along the underside of the frame and proceed to hammer home the remaining tacks. Cut off the excess calico just below the tack line, leaving the edge raw.

POSITIONING WADDING

Place a piece of sheet wadding on top of the calico,

making sure that it does not fall over the edge of the frame. If this happens the seat becomes too large for the chair frame, thus straining the chair joints. When positioning the wadding, do not cut it to size. It should be torn apart (between the fingers and thumb), which thins the edges making it blend with the other stuffing. The seat is now ready for the top cover.

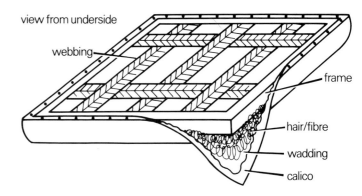

8 Right *View of layers from underside*

3 STOOLS AND LOOSE SEATS

Stools and loose seats are not always sprung, and in some cases they have a minimum of stuffing. The base can be either solid, or webbed on the top of the frame. To re-upholster a webbed frame, place a length of hessian over the seat, turn the edges up, and tack in position just inside the outer edge of the frame. The seat can now be padded by stitching ties into the hessian, stuffing with hair or fibre and covering with a layer of linter felt. On the solid seat, a layer of black felt or linter felt, covered by a layer of wadding, can be used. These 'webbed' and 'solid' methods are obviously more economical than the technique that follows, although the products are, of course, much harder to sit on.

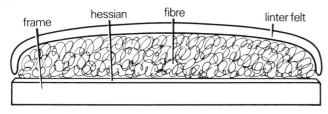

9 Section showing layers

STOOL WITH TACK ROLL

The tack roll method is used for a stool or seat that requires a built-up edge. It is a quicker alternative to making a stitched up edge (page 23). The tack roll can be used around wings, scrolls, or any edge that needs to be built up.

First web the seat (page 10) and then cut a length of hessian the same size as the seat plus 8 to 10 cm (3–4 in) extra on each side. Stretch the hessian tight across the seat, and tack in position on the edge of the frame. Starting in the middle of the back edge, take a handful of fibre and place it in a sausage shape on top of the canvas. Roll the hessian over it, packing in the stuffing as hard as possible until it makes a neat, firm roll. Then, working with about 10 cm (4 in) at a time, push the inner side of the roll against the outer edge of the frame so that it is just proud of the edge. Tack the roll in place along the inside edge of the roll.

When the corner is nearly reached, turn the extra hessian under and make a mitre on the corner. Use the regulator to ensure that the fibre is packed in evenly and

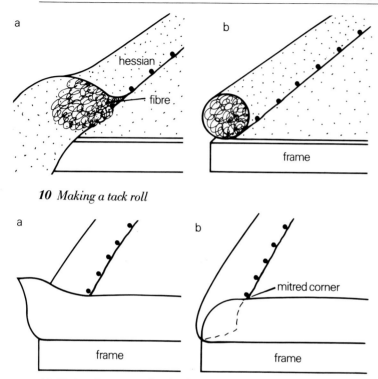

10 Making a tack roll

11 Fitting the corner of tack roll

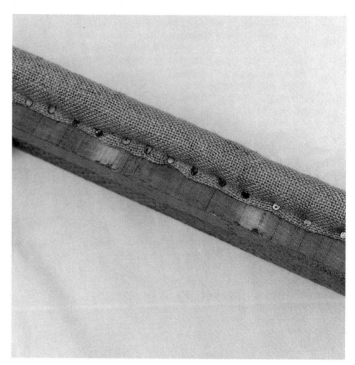

Tack roll

firmly. When the tack roll has been completed all round the edges, bridle stitch the centre section of hessian and fill with fibre until it is slightly higher than the tack roll. Cover with calico, pulling it very firmly over the edges. If the frame is show wood, finish the tack line above the rebate and cut off raw. Otherwise finish just above the lower edge. Cover the calico with a layer of wadding and the stool is ready for re-covering.

STOOL OR LOOSE SEAT USING FOAM

If the seat has rounded corners the foam must be cut 3 cm (1¼ in) wider all round and the extra 3 cm (1¼ in) should then be chamfered. But if the seat has a square edge, the foam should be cut to the exact size of the base. If the base is webbed, web and apply hessian

(pages 10–11). If it is solid, the foam can be fixed directly to the base. Using 8 cm (3 in) strips of calico with adhesive or adhesive tape, stick half the strip to the foam, leaving the other half free. On rounded edges they must be stuck to the top side of the foam, whilst on the square edge stool they must be stuck on the upright edge.

Place a tack on the halfway point of each side on the underside of the seat and work out towards each corner until the foam is smooth. Trim the excess tape or calico off at the corner. Either 13 mm (½ in) fine tacks or staples may be used, finish all round and trim off the calico at the tack line. Place a thin sheet of wadding over the foam, or, for a squashy effect, use a layer of Dacron, then re-cover.

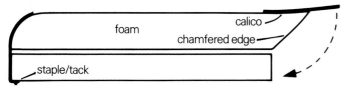

12 Making a rounded edge

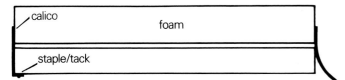

13 Making a square edge

PIN CUSHION SEAT

The pin cushion seat is usually found on small occasional chairs, stool tops and other types of show wood furniture. First the webbing is applied using 13 mm (½ in) fine tacks so as not to damage or split the frame. Web in the same manner as for the drop in seat (page 10), making sure that the webbing is on the top of the frame. Where the frame is rounded, the ends of the webbing may have to be folded at an angle so that they lie parallel to the edge of the frame (fig. 14). This also applies if the uprights are in the way of the webbing.

Having applied the webbing, cut a length of hessian to

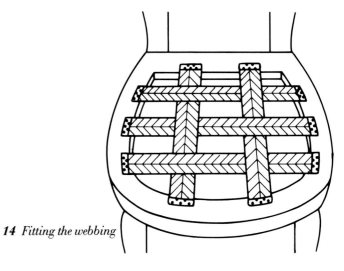

14 Fitting the webbing

cover the seat area and turnings. With the raw edge upwards, tack the hessian on to the frame, keeping inside the original hessian tack line. Turn the edges upwards. Stuff the seat with a thin layer of hair and cover it with a layer of wadding. If the fabric is very fine, use calico over the top of the hair, otherwise just cover the wadding with your chosen fabric. If calico is used, fix with very few tacks, and cut just inside the outline edge, before positioning the wadding, and finally, covering.

4 OVERSTUFF DINING CHAIR WITH SPRUNG SEAT

In the previous chapters, we dealt with simple types of seats. The re-upholstery of an overstuff seat includes all the processes involved in upholstering an easy chair seat and even larger items of furniture. If possible, practise on this type of chair before attempting a larger item, as it is much easier to handle.

We will assume that the seat needs a complete re-seat. In this case, we must remove all the old cover, stuffing, springs, and so on. Rip out in the same manner as the chair seat (page 9). After ripping out, make sure the frame is firm. If joints need re-gluing, they should be attended to at this stage. We are now ready to start the

Overstuff chair

webbing. In the case of a sprung seat, the webbing is attached to the underside of the frame. Follow the directions on page 10 for webbing a seat.

SEWING IN SPRINGS

Once the seat has been webbed, the next stage is to sew in the springs working from the underside using thread and a spring needle. First place the springs in position on top of webbing. Four springs are sufficient for an average size seat. (Five are used on a larger seat.) To start the sewing, use a slip knot. As this knot is used many times over during the upholstering, it is worth practising (fig. 15).

Stitch the twine through the material, leaving a long end and a short end. Hold on to the long end, and form the slip knot using the short end. Pull on the long end until the knot slips up tight. To lock the knot in position see fig. 15d.

Position the springs on the webbing, spaced so that they follow the frame line for maximum support. Using a spring needle and working from the underside, tie a slip knot and then make a stitch through the webbing over

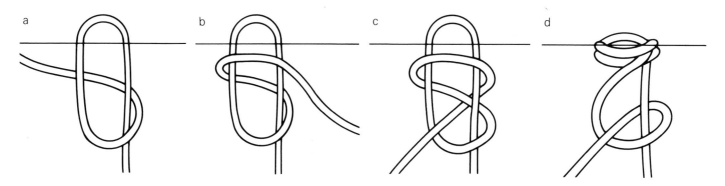

15 Above and right *Upholsterer's slip knot*

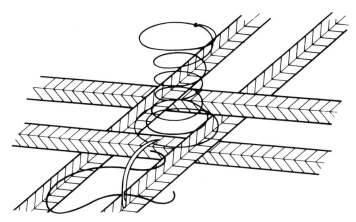

16 Sewing a spring in place

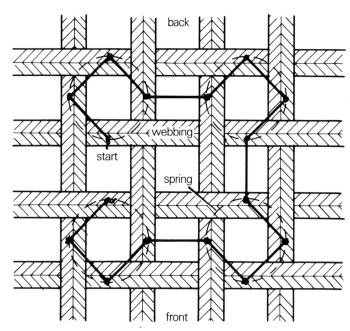

18 Stitch pattern between springs

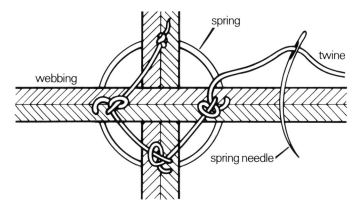

17 Stitch pattern around spring

the spring wire and back through the webbing; tie a single knot and lock it in place. Repeat on each of the four strands of web with which the spring is in contact. Proceed to stitch all the springs in place.

LASHING (LACING) THE SPRINGS

When all the springs have been stitched in place, the next stage is to lash the springs (this is sometimes called lacing). Use 16 mm (⅝ in) improved tacks and laid cord

to do this. Measure from the side edge of the frame over the top of the springs to the opposite edge, add half as much again, and cut off a piece of laid cord this length.

Place a temporary tack in one side of the frame, in line with the row of springs to be lashed. Take the length of laid cord and tie a single knot leaving enough free to stretch from the tack back to the spring. Slip the knot over the tack head, pull it tight and hammer the tack home. Leave the short end for the time being and proceed to lash down the springs with the long end in the following manner.

Compress the spring with the left hand until the initial 'give' in the spring is taken up. With the right hand, tie the first knot on the coil of the spring which is second from the top. Tie the second knot on the top coil. Stretch the cord across to the next spring, tie a knot on the top

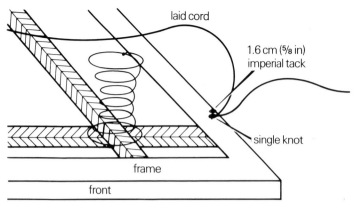

19 Attach the laid cord around a temporary tack

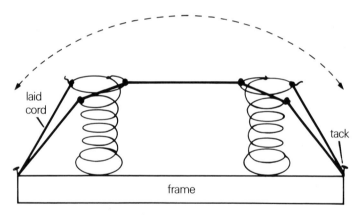

20 Laid cord lashing springs

coil of the spring, and a second on the second coil on the side closest to the frame edge. (If there are more than two springs in a row, the central springs should be tied on both sides of the top coil.) Now tap a tack into the frame and secure the laid cord by knotting it round the tack and hammering it home. Tie the loose end of the laid cord securely to the top coil of the spring (on the side closest to the frame edge). Do the same with the loose

Lashed springs on an overstuff chair

end on the first side where the tying started. It is most important that the laid cord lies in a straight line and that the springs are evenly lashed down.

Knots used in lashing springs
The hitch is the first knot used after tacking down the laid cord to the frame, it is then used alternatively with the half hitch across the seat. However, always finish with a hitch even if this means tying two hitches in a row. After tying the last knot lock it with the knot immediately below, then cut off the laid cord leaving at least 3 cm (1¼ in) of cord from the knot. There are variations on the knots shown and also varying methods of tying them. Every spring can be tied with a hitch; however,

21 *Hitch*

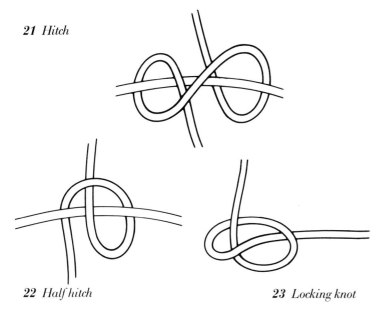

22 *Half hitch*

23 *Locking knot*

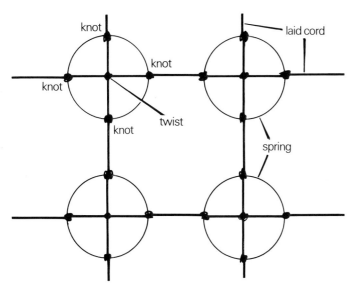

24 Above *Springs lashed in both directions*
25 Right *Fitting tarpaulin around frame upright*

alternating half-hitches with hitches is suggested because, with this method, the tension can be adjusted easily while the springs are lashed in place. (Most beginners wish they had an extra pair of hands during this process.)

Having lashed all the springs from side to side, now lash them from front to back. Where the cords cross at the centres of the springs, take a twist (fig 24). If the springs are over 22 cm (8½ in) in depth, they are lashed through the middle as well as across the top, to prevent the centre bowing out. The method used is exactly the same as the lashing already described with the only difference that the knots are tied to the middle coils on each spring.

FITTING TARPAULIN (SPRING CANVAS)

When the lashing has been completed, tarpaulin must be tacked over the springs. Cut the tarpaulin approximately 5 cm (2 in) larger overall than the area to be covered. Fold the back edge over to approximately 2.5 cm (1 in) so that the raw edge faces up. Following one thread to get a straight line, fix three temporary tacks along the centre of the back edge and stretch the tarpaulin over the springs towards the front edge. Tack in position with temporary tacks all along the back edge, and then along the side edges, smoothing the excess material towards the corners. Tack home the temporary tacks; trim off the excess material around the front and sides to approxi-

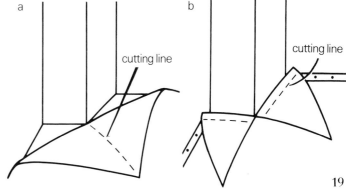

mately 2.5 cm (1 in). Where the back frame meets the seat the tarpaulin should be cut and tacked down (fig. 25).

The springs must now be stitched through the tarpaulin, using the same method as for stitching springs to the webbing. Work from spring to spring following the most logical pattern around the seat. When the stitching has been completed, finish off with a double knot. The tarpaulin is fixed on four points of the springs although if the chair has more than four springs, three fixings are sufficient, as long as they make a complete triangle. This holds the springs steady, so that they do not rub on the tarpaulin.

Now bridle stitch the tarpaulin in rows ready for stuffing. The loops should be loose enough to allow a hand to pass underneath. Follow the procedure for bridle stitching on page 11. This stitching is done over the top of the spring stitching.

FIRST STUFFING AND FITTING SCRIM

The seat is now ready for the first stuffing. Fibre is usually used for first stuffing, but hair can be used. Tease the stuffing with the fingers and then, using a handful at a time, tuck it under the loops. Start at the back, and work across and forward. Tease each handful into the next so that it masses together. Continue to cover the seat

right up to the edges. Add more to the centre section to give a domed appearance. Make sure the fibre is evenly distributed over the seat, with the outer edge of the frame just covered.

Cut a length of scrim to cover the seat plus approximately 3 cm (1¼ in) extra to tuck under, between the frame and the fibre. Starting at the back, tuck the scrim under the fibre and place a tack right on the chamfered edge of the frame. (If the frame is new it must be chamfered off on the edge, using a rasp; the edge will already be chamfered if it has been upholstered before.) Temporary tack the scrim to the middle of the back, front and each side, thus holding it in position ready for the stuffing ties.

The stuffing ties are stitched right through the seat using a double-pointed needle approximately 35 cm (14 in) long, and a strong medium twine. The pattern of stitching depends on the size and shape of the seat. On a small seat, form the stitches in a square shape following the outline of the seat. On a larger seat follow the shape illustrated in fig. 27. Starting with a slip knot, push the needle right through the seat from top to bottom, pull the needle out at the bottom, and, making a stitch approximately 1.25 cm (½ in) long, push the needle back up through the seat, then proceed to take another stitch through from the top. The top stitches should be

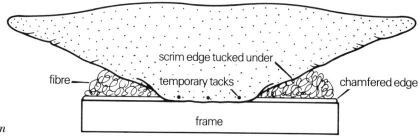

scrim edge tucked under

fibre — temporary tacks · chamfered edge

frame

26 *Positioning scrim*

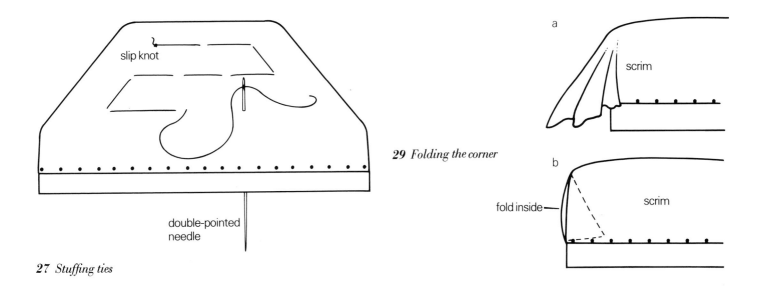

27 *Stuffing ties*

29 *Folding the corner*

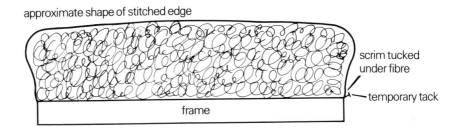

28 *Cross section with scrim in position*

approximately 15 cm (6 in). Leave the stitching loose at this stage. When the stitching is complete, start at the back and pull on the twine, while pushing the seat down. Repeat this at each stitch, until the stuffing has been pulled down as hard as possible, leaving an indentation in the centre of the seat. When the last stitch has been reached, tie the loose end round the last stitch and knot off the twine. (Do not come out to the edge of the seat with this stitch; leave at least a 10 cm [4 in] margin.)

Ease the scrim over the fibre towards the front of the frame and tuck the excess under the fibre. To obtain the right tension takes a good deal of practise. The object is to have the scrim tight enough to enable the edge to be stitched, but not so tight that it flattens out the edge. Find the approximate position of where the stitched edge will be and pinch between thumb and forefinger to form a roll. Use this method at the front and back and both sides to gauge the tension of the scrim. Temporary tack the scrim to the frame at the back, sides and front, working from the centres towards the corners. Fold the corners under to form a good square corner exactly in line with the corner of the frame.

USING THE REGULATOR

When the stuffing ties have been completed and the scrim has been tacked down, the stuffing must be 'regulated'. This means that, using a regulator, the stuffing is distributed to exactly the area where it is needed. To use the regulator on the edge, hold the edge between the thumb and fingers, and place the point of the regulator into the stuffing a few centimetres away from the fingers. By twisting the regulator back and forth, the stuffing will be pulled towards the edge, thus making it very firm. The fingers and thumb are used to feel the stuffing and to make sure it is being regulated evenly.

BLIND STITCHING

When the stuffing is firmly in place along the top edge, the next step is to blind stitch the edges. Use the 20 cm (8 in) double-pointed needle, and thread it with a fairly long length of twine. Start at the back left of the seat and work forward, inserting the needle as low down as possible, close in to the frame, and pushing it at an angle

until it comes out approximately 10 cm (4 in) from the top edge of the seat. Pull the needle *nearly* out, then push it back into the seat, so that it comes out on the bottom edge approximately 2 cm (¾ in) to the left of where it was inserted. With the two loose ends, make a slip knot and pull tight.

Form the next stitch by inserting the needle 3 cm (1¼ in) to the right and repeating the procedure. When the needle is halfway out, take the twine on the left side and wind it round the needle for three turns. Continue to pull the needle out, and then place it out of the way on the worktop (it is not necessary to unthread it). Pull the twine first to the left and then to the right, until it is as tight as possible. To prevent the twine from cutting the hands wear an old leather glove on the right hand. At the corner let the needle come out through the same point at the top until the corner has been turned. Continue to blind stitch all round the edge of the seat. The blind stitching will have moved the stuffing towards the edges, so use the regulator again.

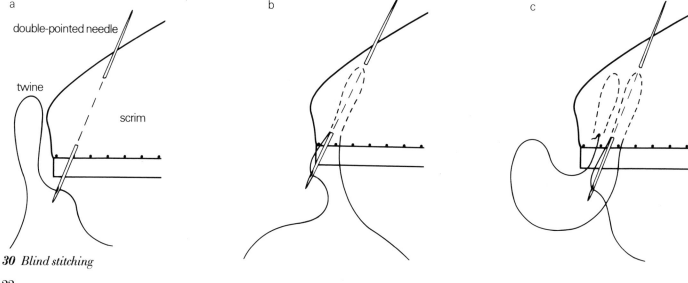

a
double-pointed needle
twine
scrim
b
c

30 *Blind stitching*

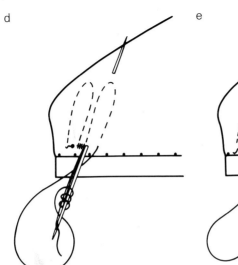

Blind stitching continued

THE STITCHED EDGE

To form the stitched edge, the method is almost the same as the blind stitch with the difference that, instead of leaving the needle in the seat at the top edge, the needle is pulled right out and then placed in the seat about 2 cm (¾ in) to the left, thus forming a stitch. When this is pulled tight it begins to form the stitched edge. Start the stitching about 1.25 cm (½ in) above the blind stitching and come through on the top surface of the seat approximately 8 cm (3 in) from the front edge. The second row of stitching should start about 3 cm (1¼ in) above the first row and on the top surface, the row of

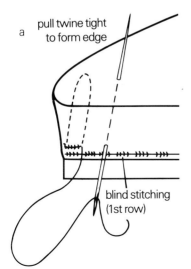

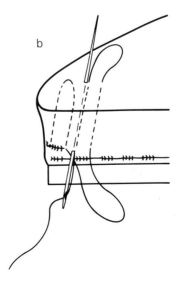

31 Edge Stitching

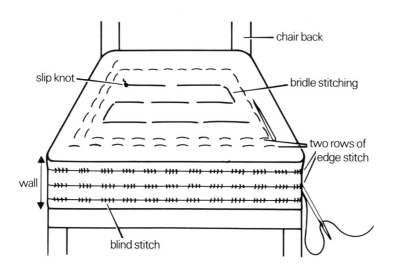

32 Blind stitch and first row of edge stitch complete

Layer of stuffing on overstuff chair

stitches should be about 4 cm (1½ in) inside the first row. Two rows of stitching will normally be sufficient but to make the wall higher, three may be necessary. Finish the stitching all round the edges. The edge should now be very hard and rigid. Proceed with the second stuffing.

Sew bridle stitching across the seat in the same way as for the first stuffing. Proceed to stuff handfuls of hair under the stitching until the whole seat area is evenly covered right to the edge of the seat. Now the seat is ready for covering with calico.

COVERING WITH CALICO

Cut a length of calico to cover the seat and to reach down the sides, front and back. Starting from the middle of the back, place a temporary tack through the calico and into the frame, and pull the calico over towards the front centre. Hammer in a tack to hold it in place, before repeating the process from side to side. (By pushing with one hand and pulling with the other, make the calico as tight as possible.) Working from the centre of each side

'Up to calico' on overstuff chair

Covered and finished overstuff chair

out towards the corners, cut into the back corners and fasten in place with temporary tacks. At the front corners pull down at the centre point and hold with a temporary tack. Then ease the excess fabric into small pleats. An alternative way of finishing the corner is to cut the excess fabric away leaving just sufficient for the raw edges to meet. This is called butting and it gives a square corner.

Once the corner has been completed, the temporary tacks can be tacked home, and the calico trimmed back almost to the edge of the tack line, leaving a raw edge. A layer of wadding should now be placed on the seat, two layers of sheet wadding may be used if it seems thin. This prevents the hair penetrating through to the top cover. Trim the wadding to within 5 cm (2 in) of the frame by pulling between the thumb and fingers. (It must not be cut as this makes an impression right through the top cover.) It is important to leave the wadding short of the

frame because when the top cover is pulled over, the padding will be pulled down to the edge. The seat is now ready for its top cover.

HELPFUL TIPS

If the corners of a frame are in bad shape, a piece of buckram or card can be tacked in place. To square a corner, position it under the stitched edge, leaving it shy of the frame at the bottom edge.

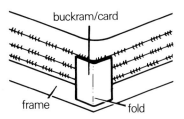

33 Squaring the corner

5 RE-SEATING AN EASY CHAIR

The processes used in the re-seating of an easy chair are identical to those used for the overstuff seat, right up to the fitting of the tarpaulin. (Note that cushion seats require level springing and full seats require springing that is 4 cm [1½ in] higher at the centre than it is at the front edge.)

Fit the tarpaulin to the lower rail on the sides and back and to the upper rail on the front. Cut the tarpaulin where it meets the upright rails and turn it back 1.25 cm (½ in). Tack the tarpaulin in place in the same way as for the overstuff chair (page 19). Follow the procedures for sewing the springs to the tarpaulin, and bridle stitch ready for the first stuffing on page 20.

Next, stuff the seat with fibre allowing it to go just under the top rail, and right up to the front edge on the

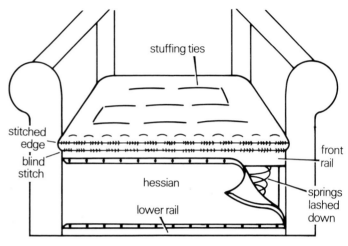

35 *Front edge stitched up; hessian almost tacked in place*

front rail. When the stuffing is complete, place the scrim on the lower rail using temporary tacks, pull the scrim over the stuffing in the front, tuck under and temporary tack in place.

Stuffing ties should now be sewn right through the seat (page 20). Adjust and tack all the tacks home round the sides and back.

Make sure there is enough stuffing on the front edge. If there is not, add more at this stage by removing the temporary tacks and adding an extra handful of fibre, or more, until the correct effect is achieved. Replace tacks and tack home.

Blind stitch the front edge, regulate the stuffing and then stitch the front edge so that it is very firm and even in depth (pages 22–23).

When the front edge has been completed, cut a length of hessian to fit over the gap between the top and lower rail. Turn the edges back so that the raw edges face front and tack in position (fig. 35).

Bridle stitch the seat in the same way as for the first

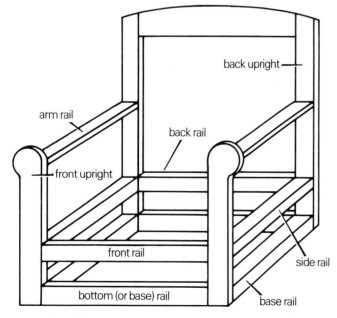

34 *Easy chair frame*

stuffing and proceed with the second stuffing. Allow the stuffing to reach just to the frame edge on the side. Cut a length of calico, enough to cover right over the seat area and over the front edge. Tack it to the back rail and to the side rails. Pull the calico over the front edge and tack it onto the front top rail. The edge of the calico must be left raw. Finally, cut the excess away from the corners of the front edge and tack home.

Stitch bridle ties onto the front border, and stuff the whole area with a thin layer of hair. Cover with a length of calico and attach it to either side of the uprights. The seat is now ready to be re-covered (Chapter 13).

Tweed armchair

6 EASY CHAIR WITH SPRUNG BACK, SPRUNG ARMS AND INDEPENDENT SPRUNG FRONT EDGE

This type of chair is one of the most difficult to do, but one of the most comfortable available. Use the best materials that you can afford, because even though they cannot be seen under the cover, this foundation is most important. The use of a good wadding directly beneath the cover not only stops the hair coming through, but also stops the cover from wearing. A cover can wear out just as quickly from the inside, especially if it is a pile fabric which has an abrasive material under it. The

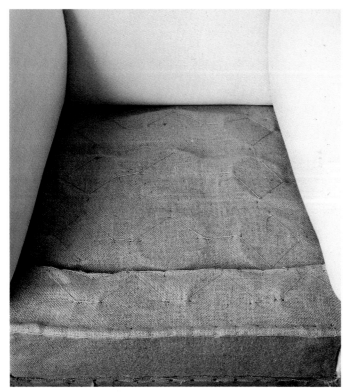

Independent front edge

abrasive stuffing wears the pile away from its backing and makes the pile fall out.

There are a number of chairs and settees which have not been stuffed with hair. The variety of stuffings in old chairs ranges from alva (seaweed) to rag flock, wood wool and so on. Stuffings and fillings are being improved and experimented with and, in time, many of the old materials will disappear. (Some are already difficult to obtain.) For this reason, it is important to try some of the new types of stuffing as well as the traditional ones. This does not mean that I recommend substituting the original materials on a Victorian chair for a piece of foam. However, duck down for instance has become so expensive that many people are using a foam substance wrapped in a fibrefill material for seat or back cushions. The effect has the feel of a soft and squashy cushion.

On a clean frame, the arms are attended to first (because they are less accessible once the seat is finished), then comes the seat and finally the back. However, it is not always necessary to re-upholster the entire chair. The seat is the most likely area to require attention and, therefore, this is the step described first.

THE INDEPENDENT SPRUNG EDGE
This type of chair has springs set on the front edge of the frame to give a softer seat. The main part of the seat is webbed, stitched and lashed in exactly the same manner as the overstuff dining chair (Chapter 4). Place the spring canvas over the seat springs allowing enough extra to cover the front springs and to form a gutter between the seat springs and the front edge.

Using 15 cm (6 in) by 8 gauge springs, (four or five are usually sufficient), place the springs level with the

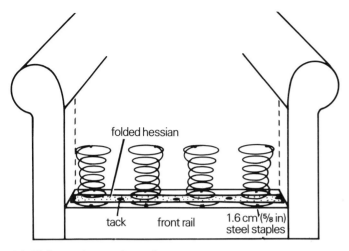

36 Fixing springs on front edge

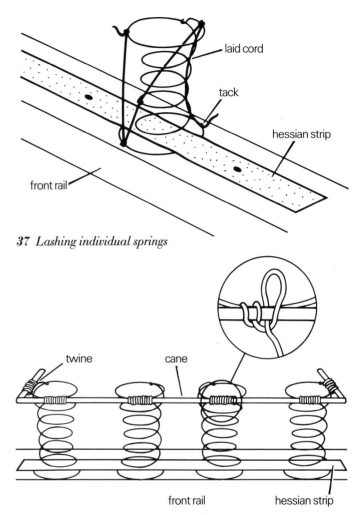

37 Lashing individual springs

38 Cane bent to shape and bound to springs

front edge of the frame. Fix in position using 1.5 cm (⅝ in) steel staples. Lay a double thickness strip of hessian (or webbing folded in half lengthwise to a width of 4 cm [1½ in]) along the length of the front rail so that it passes through the spring lying across the bottom coil. Place a tack in between each spring through the hessian into the front rail and tack home. The hessian prevents the coils from hitting the front rail and making a clattering noise when someone sits down.

Use your hand to compress each spring to a height just below the level of the seat springs. Lash each spring into position using laid cord following this procedure. Fix a temporary 16 mm (⅝ in) imperial tack on the inside of the front rail directly behind one of the springs. Attach a length of laid cord to the rack and hammer home. Take the laid cord up through the spring and knot on the inner side of the middle coil. Take to the inner side of the top coil and knot again. Now bring the laid cord through the spring down to the outer side of the middle coil and knot. Follow down to the bottom coil, knot and then fix a final knot on the outer side of the top coil (fig. 37).

Once the springs have been lashed down, a length of

cane must be bent in shape to fit along the front edge and width of the front rail. Sometimes, a heavy gauge wire is used instead of cane. Now bind the cane to the top coil of each spring using a medium-weight twine. (Follow the binding process illustrated in fig. 38.)

Having bound the cane to the springs, the next step is to make a gutter between the seat and the spring edge, so that the front edge remains independent. To do this, tuck the spring canvas that is already attached to the seat down between the seat and front edge. This gutter is held in place by fixing a length of laid cord from the side rail across the gutter and on to the opposite side rail. Loop each end of the laid cord round 16 mm (⅝ in) imperial tacks, and tack home. Fold the spring canvas back over the laid cord and at a point between each spring make a hole through the canvas using the regulator. Thread a length of laid cord through the hole and tie with a slip knot, so that the knot holds the laid cord in the gutter firmly together with the canvas. Place two of these ties between each spring, and secure them by tacking them to the top of the front edge.

After completing the gutter ties, pull the spring canvas forward over the spring edge and temporary tack halfway down the front rail to allow room for the turn under. Fold the edge under and tack down. The spring canvas must now be attached to the outer side of the springs by using a medium twine to stitch through the canvas and catch both the top coil and the cane. (See stitched edge on page 23.)

Now sew bridle ties over the whole seat area (page 11) and insert stuffing under the ties. Fill in the gutter with stuffing also, until the whole seat has an even layer of hair or fibre across it. At this stage, a length of scrim must be cut to fit right over the seat from the back rail to the front edge leaving enough to tuck under. Fold the scrim under approximately 1.25 cm (½ in) and temporary tack along the middle of the top side of the back rail. Pull the scrim over the hair or fibre and tack down on the two side rails. Keep the threads of the scrim straight, from front to back and from side to side. Then, starting in the centre of the front edge, fold the scrim under and tuck it beneath the stuffing along the front edge. Use a

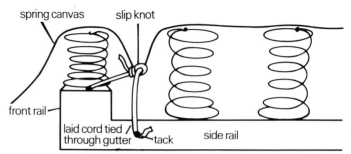

39 *Side section; fixing laid cord in the gutter*

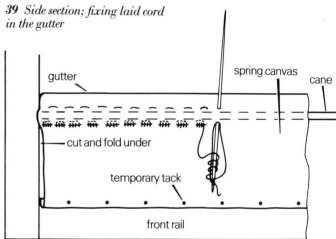

40 *Stitching front edge*

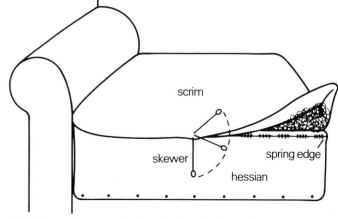

41 *Using a skewer, push the scrim into the front edge*

skewer to hold it in place. (To use a skewer, push it into the scrim, lever it down, then push it up into place so that it holds firm.)

Having tucked the scrim under the front edge, it must now be secured to the hessian using a blanket stitch. But first, before starting the blanket stitch, sew the stuffing ties through the seat so that you will not be caught out if the skewers need adjustment.

Now blind stitch (pages 22–23) the front edge and then stitch it up with one row of running stitches. Continue to finish in the same manner as for the overstuff chair up to the point where calico is fitted over the front edge. When fitting calico to an independent edge, it cannot be tacked to the frame. Instead, you should follow this procedure. Pull the calico over the edge, ease the fullness on the corners and proceed to stitch right through the calico into the front edge, using a strong twine and a circular needle. The stitch used is a long running stitch. Secure the twine at the beginning and at the end of the border, and cut off excess calico. Pad the front border section and slip stitch down under the lip. Tack the rest of the front edge in the same way as for the overstuff chair (pages 24–25).

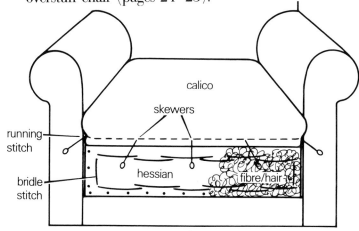

42 *Stuffing the front edge*

THE INDEPENDENT SPRUNG ARM

To make a sprung arm, first tack two pieces of webbing vertically on to the inside of the frame. The piece nearest the inside back should be folded in half, and placed about 5 cm (2 in) from the frame edge, this gives a line to the inside arm and allows the outer cover to be pulled through at a later stage. The other piece of webbing should be placed approximately half-way along the arm stretching from the top rail to bottom rail.

Before positioning the springs place a strip of folded hessian or a length of webbing, folded in half, along the length of the arm frame and tack down diagonally. This step helps prevent the springs clattering against the

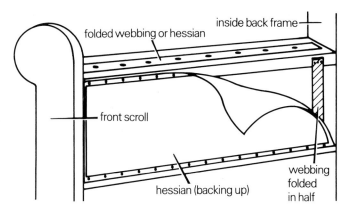

43 *Backing up the arm*

frame. After fixing the webbing, place a length of hessian on the frame, and tack home, this is called 'backing up' (fig. 43).

A much lighter spring is used for the arm (12.5 cm [5 in] by 12 gauge) is sufficient. Staple (using galvanized staples) the springs on the lowest coil of each spring, in line with the front scroll. Usually, five springs are placed along this rail. If the springs are wider than the rail, the lower coil is bent over the edge and stapled down.

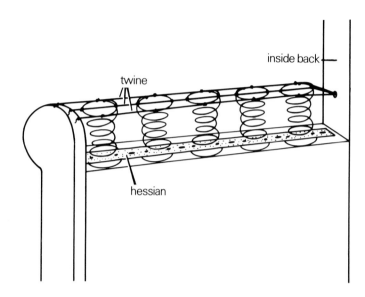

44 *Lashing springs*

The next stage is to lash the springs with three lines stretching the length of the arm. Starting with the centre line, fix a temporary tack into the inside back upright, loop the twine around it and hammer it home. Draw the twine in a line across the centre of the springs fastening with a knot on each top coil at front and back, and secure around a tack on the front scroll (fig. 44). Use a spring twine (heavy gauge) and tie the knots illustrated on page 16. The spring is not held down very tight and it should be just above the level of the front scroll.

Now cut a length of hessian 8 cm (3 in) longer than the arm and wide enough to cover from the bottom of the inside arm rail over the springs to the bottom outside arm rail, allowing an extra 6 cm (2½ in) for turning. Starting on the inside, temporary tack the hessian along the rail. Then pull the hessian over the top of the springs and temporary tack on the outer side of the rail. Keep the hessian taut by placing a temporary tack in line with the outer lashing both at the scroll and at the back. Adjust the tacks, if necessary, and tack home on the arm rail

both sides.

The lines of twine are now completely enclosed in hessian, and must be stitched in place. Using a blanket stitch, put the needle through the hessian catching in the lashing twine which runs along the edge of the springs. Trap the twine as the blanket stitch proceeds, and catch in the edge of each spring as you come to it. Carry out this stitching on each of the outside edges to make a good boxed shape. Now sew in bridle stitches and start to stuff with fibre. The stitching prevents the stuffing from being displaced in wear.

Tuck the hessian under the edge of the scroll, adding extra stuffing if needed. Tack in place. Blind stitch round the edge and then top stitch, using the regulator to keep stuffing even and hard (fig. 46). The position of this stitched edge depends on whether the scroll is on the edge or under the edge. For the under-edge scroll add more stuffing and let the stitched edge stand proud of the frame. For the edge scroll the stuffing stays level with the scroll.

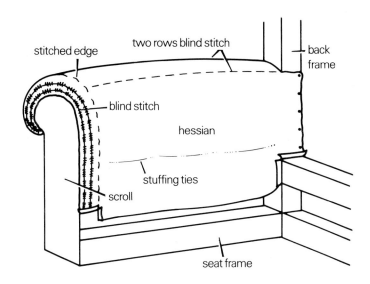

45 Inside arm ready for second stuffing

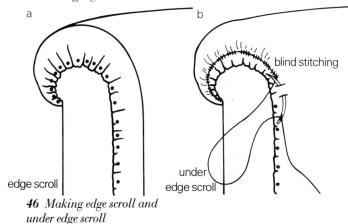

46 Making edge scroll and under edge scroll

The arm is now bridle stitched and a second stuffing has been added. Cover the whole arm in calico, temporary tacking it at the back, on the arm rail and on the side rail. Draw the calico over the front of the arm. If the chair has an edge scroll the calico can be pleated in and then tacked in place taking care to keep a good outline on the outer edge. On an under-edge scroll, the calico is secured with skewers, and a row of blind stitching is sewn through the stitched edge as close to the frame as possible. You can use either a curved or cording needle for this and fine twine. Pull the twine just hard enough to secure the calico, without disturbing the stuffing. Trim away the excess calico, and drive home the tacks on the rails. A layer of wadding is added just before re-covering (fig. 47).

THE INDEPENDENT SPRUNG BACK

Starting from the bottom rail, evenly space the vertical strips of webbing following the frame line. (The distance between each strip should be approximately the width of a piece of webbing.) Tack in place on the outside of the bottom rail and on the inside of the top rail. Use the web stretcher for this step and tack in a staggered formation (page 10). Weave in four horizontal strips of webbing. Place two of these close together near the bottom rail as this takes the bulk of the wear. Place the remaining two above the arm frame (do not web in between the arm

33

frames as this blocks the passage of the fabric when re-covering). Tack each end of the web strips on to the outside of the back verticals in a staggered formation.

Springs

The method for sewing the springs in place is the same as for the seat. The springs are sewn on from the back of the webbing (fig. 47). A strong gauge spring (15 cm [6 in] × 10 gauge) would be used for the bottom row and a lighter gauge (17 cm [7 in] × 12 gauge) for the two top rows. Nine springs are sufficient for an average-sized chair.

The springs must now be lashed on the front to hold them in place. The three heavy springs at the bottom are lashed from side to side with laid cord in the same way as for the overstuff dining chair (page 18). The remaining springs are tied in place with twine following the pattern shown in fig. 48. Starting at the spring on the top left, fix a tack towards the end of the top rail. Secure the twine around this, then take a twist around the centre coil of the spring and attach the other end to a second tack placed in a position the same distance from the centre of the spring as the first tack. Repeat for the other two springs on the top row. Use the same principle for the second row, except that on the two side springs, fix the first tack to the side rail rather than the top rail.

Now the springs are in position and the back is ready for the spring canvas. From this point the processes for stuffing and stitching the edge are exactly the same as for the overstuff seat (pages 19–24). Once the second stuffing is complete, cover the back with calico and wadding. The back is now ready to re-cover.

springs
sewn in
from
back

seat area

47 Springs sewn on to webbing from back

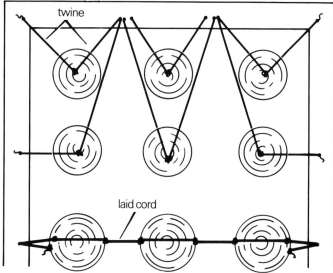

twine

laid cord

48 Lashing back springs

A collection of furniture covered with traditional fabrics

7 WINGS AND FACINGS

WINGS

With the traditional method of upholstery the wings are 'built up' to the covering stage, whereas with the modern method they are either cut to size in foam or rubberized hair, or simply padded with a layer of linter felt or black felt. If you are following the modern method the padding can be left until you start the final covering.

To build a wing by the traditional method, first cut a length of webbing to fill the gap in the frame. This is placed near to the back, so that the cover may be pulled through past this web (fig. 49). Fold the webbing in half down its length before tacking into place. A length of hessian is then cut and stretched across the opening, turn the edges back and tack to three sides leaving the back loose. Thread the hessian through the gap between the inside wing and inside back (you can sew it to the webbing). If a tack roll is appropriate for the wing, make it now (pages 13–14). Finally, the wing can be filled with fibre and a layer of linter felt following one of two procedures:

1 Bridle stitch the hessian, tease in the fibre under these ties, and cover with scrim. Place a stuffing tie through the wing, and then proceed to make the stitched edge in the same manner as for the overstuff seat (page 23). One blind stitch and one edge stitch will generally be sufficient. Finish the wing with a layer of hair, fibre or linter felt.
2 A slim solid wing simply needs a piece of linter felt laid directly on the hessian of the wing. The final fabric can then be shaped and pulled straight over this padding, and secured in place with tacks.

On some modern chairs where the wing has been glued and screwed on to the chair after the back has been covered, it is very difficult to remove the wing without

damage. If this is the case, the inside back should be covered first and then enough fabric should be cut for the wing to allow for back tacking into the frame. Back tack by placing a plastic strip or strip of card on the wrong side of the fabric in line with the hem edge (fig. 50). Make sure that the fabric is kept upright and the pattern runs straight across in line with the inside back. Now tack the backing strip through the fabric and into the frame upright. When this has been completed, the wing can be padded with a layer of linter felt plus a thin layer of wadding. Then cover the wing (page 59).

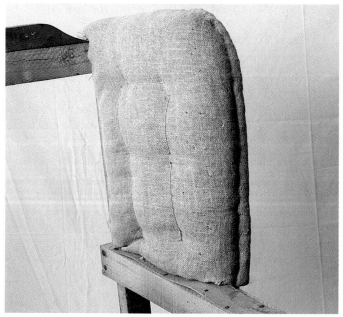

Old-fashioned wing covered with hessian and stitched with bridle ties

49 Opposite right *Tack a folded length of webbing to inside arm*
50 Opposite far right *Fitting fabric using plastic back tack strip*

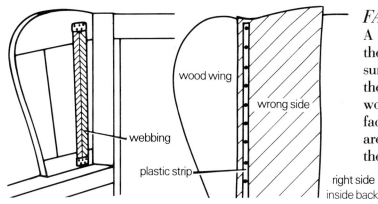

labels: wood wing, wrong side, webbing, plastic strip, right side, inside back

FACINGS

A front facing can be cut from plywood and bolted onto the front of the frame. The bolt hole must be counter-sunk from the front using a drill. Attach the bolt pad and then apply the final cover. With the exception of the wooden or cardboard facings, most of the scrolls and soft facings are either machined in with the arm cover or they are slipped in place after the arms are finished. In each of these cases they would be padded at the time of covering.

8 CONSTRUCTING A DEEP-BUTTON-BACKED HEADBOARD

A deep-button-backed headboard can be made to any shape required. The headboard here uses a basic method to construct a fairly simply shape. If the shape is too fussy it will detract from the button work.

First measure the width and height required. Draw a shape on a piece of brown paper and place it behind the bed. Raise or lower it until the height looks right, then mark the paper where the top edge of the mattress meets it. This is the point at which padding will begin.

Take a length of 1.25 cm (½ in) chipboard or ply board (for a double headboard use 2 cm (¾ in) chip-board) and use the template to cut the headboard. Measuring from the mark on the template, leave 15 cm (6 in) extra on the lower edge to go down behind the mattress. Now, lay the template on a sheet of 8 cm (3 in) foam and draw round the shape (do not add the extra 15 cm [6 in] this time.) When the shape has been drawn, measure 3 cm (1¼ in) from the line all the way round and draw a second line, this one is to be the cutting line. Cut the foam using a sharp knife. An electric carving knife is very useful for this purpose in the absence of a foam cutter.

The board must now be marked ready to drill holes for the buttons. First measure across the board and mark the middle. Draw a line vertically up through this point. Measure from the 15 cm (6 in) mark to the top of the board, mark halfway and draw a line horizontally forming a cross. Mark the centre with a circle. The headboard can be buttoned in large or small diamonds, depending on the size and depth of the board, and, of course, on personal choice. An average size of 15 cm (6 in) marked on the board makes a diamond of approximately 10 cm (4 in) from outer edge to outer edge. Mark the board in the following manner.

Draw horizontal lines on the board at 8 cm (3 in) intervals. Then mark intervals along each horizontal line. Make the first points at a 8 cm (3 in) distance each side of the centre vertical. Then progress along the horizontal with a point at 15 cm (6 in) intervals. After marking in all along the lines, use a straight edge to draw a diagonal line through the marks from left to right, then from right to left (fig. 52). Continue to draw the lines across. The point at which they cross each other is the point at which the buttons will be positioned. The board is ready to be

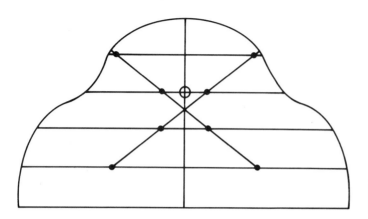

51 Draw the first two diagonals

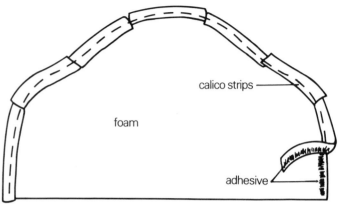

53 Glueing calico strips to foam

calico strips

foam

adhesive

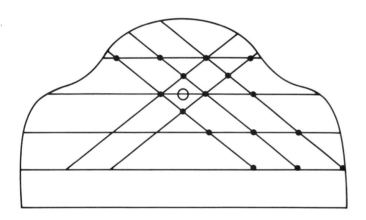

52 Lines marked at regular intervals

drilled as soon as the marking is complete. The drill hole should be large enough to allow a mattress needle and thread through, 3 mm (⅛ in). Drill the holes right through the board, and make sure that they are at the centre of each cross. If the button marks are near the edge, drill to the nearest within 5 cm (2 in) of the edge.

Once the holes are drilled the next stage is to prepare the foam, for good deep effect at least 8 cm (3 in) foam

should be used. For a small area, however, quite a good effect can be achieved with 5 cm (2 in) foam. Now the 3 cm (1¼ in) margin on the foam must be champhered off to fit the board. To do this cut a line from the outer edge of the foam diagonally across to meet the 3 cm (1¼ in) margin line. Next, cut some strips of calico to approximately 8 cm (3 in) wide. Cut a snip in the edge and tear the calico across so that it does not make a sharp edge under the cover. Arrange the strips around the outer edge of the foam, overlapping on to the foam by approximately half the width of the strip. If the foam is curved in shape, overlap each section (fig. 53) so that the outer edge is covered. Using a good adhesive, spread it across half the width of the calico strip and the same distance in from the outer edge of the foam. Press the two together, and leave to dry.

Centre the top edge and place a temporary tack in the back of the board. Repeat at the centre of the two sides, pulling the calico until the outer edge of the foam covers the outer edge of the board. Temporary tack in position until the foam is lying smoothly. To ease round the corners, gather the calico into small pleats and tack down. If the foam is pulled too hard it will result in a 'girt'. If this happens release the tack from the calico until the girt disappears. When satisfied, tack home and trim the calico off to the tack line, snipping the edge to aid the fit.

With a mattress needle, mark the hole through the foam by pushing the needle through from the back of the board. Where it appears on the foam, make a cross cut, this helps to eliminate resistance when buttoning. The headboard can now be finished with the final covering (page 65).

9 DEEP-BUTTON-BACKED, IRON-FRAME CHAIR

The deep-button-backed chair is usually the one that beginners choose to tackle. My advice is to start on something simple and master the basic stitching first. This type of chair has a wooden base frame, and so the seat can be re-upholstered using the methods described on pages 26–27. This will bring the seat up to the calico stage. The back of the chair, however, is made entirely of iron, therefore everything on this part of the chair has to be hand-stitched in place.

Before deciding if the chair needs re-upholstering or just re-covering, remove the old cover by cutting the button ties and stitching which hold the cover in place, inspect the scrim, the hessian and the stuffing. If the stitched edge is not worn and the back hessian is not torn, then the chair will only need re-covering. Keep the old cover so that the button markings can be used for a guide. (Do not, however, use as a pattern but rather, to measure distances.) Then turn to page 70 for the re-covering procedure. If you decide that the whole chair needs re-upholstering, the first step is to strip it right back to the frame. Save the hair, as this can be teased out and re-used. (Repair the frame at this stage if necessary.)

Start by cutting strips of hessian or calico approximately 5 cm (2 in) wide. These strips are used to bind the frame which provides a base on which to sew, and also stops the metal from wearing the hessian foundation. The binding should be left raw on the edges, and should

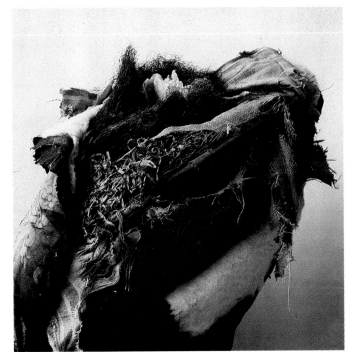

Ripping out an iron-frame chair

overlap on each turn. Secure the binding lengths with a few stitches at each end. The uprights and horizontals should be bound first, then turn to the outer edges of the frame.

After the frame has been bound, cut a length of

39

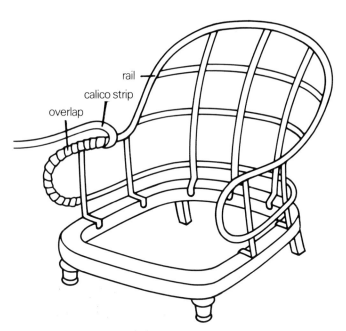

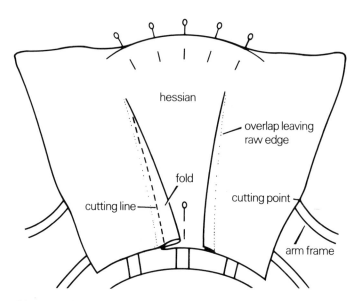

55 *Fitting hessian to inside back*

54 *Iron-frame chair*

hessian sufficient to cover the entire back, with enough allowance, approximately 6 cm (2½ in), to turn over the top and bottom edges. Place the hessian on the front side of the frame (some upholsterers prefer to place it on the outside of the frame), and with the grain of the fabric running upright, turn it right over the top edge until it meets under the frame rail. Secure with skewers, and then repeat along the top edge until the inside back meets the arm uprights. Secure the centre of the hessian to the bottom rail with skewers in the same manner as you secured the top. The hessian will be full at this stage, so to mould it to the shape of the back, two cuts must be made. Starting from the bottom, cut approximately two-thirds up the hessian to cut out the fullness. To bring the hessian round to the back, cut it at the point at which the frame curves toward the arms. Having made the cuts,

overlap the edges of hessian so that the piece lies flat. Trim back the excess leaving approximately 5 cm (2 in) under the overlap. Secure the hessian under the bottom rail keeping it taut between top and bottom.

After positioning the hessian on the back, use exactly the same method to cover the arms, overlapping the hessian where the back and arm sections meet. Skewer the hessian in place, and then starting at the lower edge, sew all round the outside edge of the frame. Keep the stitch line close to the frame so that it does not allow any movement, which ultimately causes wear. Use a medium twine and a spring needle to form either a running stitch or a locking stitch (preferably the locking stitch—see fig. 57).

To ensure a firm foundation for the stuffing, a stitched-up edge should be made from the point where the arms meet the seat, all round the top edge of the frame. To make the stitched edge, cut strips of scrim approximately 20 cm (8 in) wide. Fold one edge under

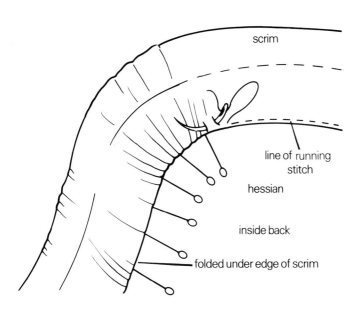

56 Fitting scrim around frame back

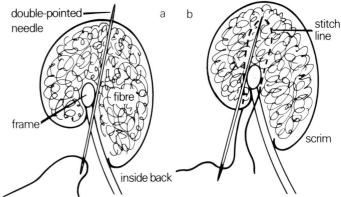

57 Sections showing position of blind stitch

1.5 cm (⅝ in). Measure about 8 cm (3 in) down from the top of the frame edge and draw a line following the contour of the frame. Fold the scrim under at this line and stitch all round on the same line. Allow extra on the open curves and ease in on the closed curves, to allow the scrim to fold over the top of the frame without distortion.

Complete the stitching all round, then taking a handful of fibre, pack it into the scrim. Pull the scrim over the back edge of the frame, thus forming a roll over the outer edge. Tuck the ends of the scrim under and secure with skewers just under the frame. Continue to make the roll by adding more fibre. Keep the roll evenly packed and regulate the stuffing at intervals so that no lumps are formed. When the roll is in position, use a double-pointed needle and twine to sew a blind stitch right through the roll on the underside of the metal frame coming out again with the needle over the top of the frame. The blind stitch will secure the scrim to the

hessian on the outside back during this process.

(When upholstering a wooden frame, spoon back chair, the hessian is tacked to the back edge of the frame and the edge stitched to follow the outline of the frame.)

Once the blind stitch has been completed all round, move on to the stitched edge. Stitch just above the blind stitch on the outside back, keeping the needle to the back edge of the frame. (See stitched edge on page 23.) Once the edge is stitched the next stage is to make a swell in the lower part of the inside back.

Draw a semi-circle measuring approximately 25 cm (10 in) from the bottom frame to the centre of the circle and graduating to nothing where the back joins the arms (fig. 59). Fill this area with bridle stitching. Now cut a length of scrim large enough to cover the area plus an allowance of 15 cm (6 in) all round to enable it to cover the stuffing. Turn the scrim under on the top edge and stitch to the curve of the swell. Stuff fibre under the bridle stitches until the area is firm. Pull the scrim over the swell and under the frame line to the outside back. Cut away the scrim where it is trapped by the upright. From the outside back, sew the scrim on to the foundation hessian using a running stitch.

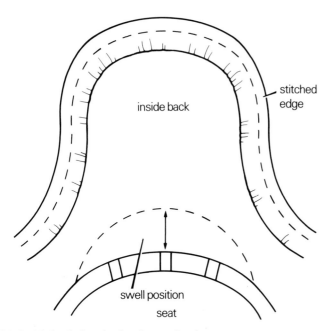

58 Inside back showing hessian and scrim

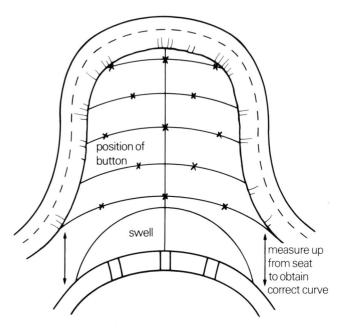

59 Marking the chair back for buttons

Now that the swell is completed, the position of the buttons should be marked. Using a needle and thread, mark from the front side, right through so that they can be seen clearly from the back of the hessian. A pattern of three, two, three is a fairly common one (that is to say, three buttons at the top, two in the centre, then three again and so on). To establish the position of the buttons, draw a vertical line down the centre of the chair back; cross this with another line across the top of the swell, keeping it even by taking the measurement up from the seat. Measure four more lines up from the bottom line, with a distance of 9 cm (3½ in) between each line. (This is an average measurement, it will vary depending on the size of the chair. The number of buttons different chairs require will also vary.)

At this stage, the arms, too, should be marked for buttons. Generally, one button is placed in the centre, and one where the arm meets the back; these are in line with the lowest row of buttons on the back of the chair. Bridle stitch the arms and back, tease the hair and stuff under the ties until it feels firm. Push the regulator through from the back and break open the hair. Add a layer of wadding and then break holes in this layer. At this point, the back and arms may be covered in calico, particularly if the top cover is a fine fabric. Now follow the instructions for top covering (Chapter 17).

Covered iron-frame chair

PART II
COVERING AND RE-COVERING

10 TYPES OF FABRIC FOR COVERING

Ambla: a laminated fabric which has the look of leather, but is much cheaper and also easier to clean.

Brocade: made in silk, cotton and man-made fibres, this fabric has an embroidered look with a sheen on the surface. The designs are usually traditional. It is not recommended for very hard wear.

Brocatelle: a fairly heavy fabric, with a silky look. The design is woven in and looks padded. Made in cotton, silk, man-made fibres or a mixture of both man-made and natural fibre.

Calico: a fine cotton fabric, made in different weights, and used unbleached as under covering.

Chintz: cotton fabric with a heavy glazed surface. Suitable for areas where it will have fairly light wear.

Cirrus: a man-made, leather-look cloth, in a great variety of colours and finishes.

Damask: a self-patterned fabric achieved by reversing the weave on the back to produce a light and shade effect. Available in silk, cotton, rayon and terylene.

Hide: this is usually cow hide which can be dyed to a variety of shades and is very hard-wearing as long as it is not allowed to dry out. Hide food or wax polish will keep the hide supple. It is sold by the square foot.

Linen: linen and linen union are often used for loose covers because of their washing qualities.

Moquette: a looped, pile fabric with loops that can be cut or uncut, or a combination of both. It is very hard-wearing and made in wool, cotton or man-made fibres.

Tapestry: if it is hand-made in wool on a linen backing it will wear for many years. Most tapestry, however, is made by machine, in cotton, wool, and worsted yarn. Many designs are traditional, although modern designs are available.

Tweed: a woven fabric which can be heavy or light-weight. Different effects are achieved by a variety of yarn thickness. Made in wool or mixed with a man-made yarn, it is hard-wearing.

Velour and velvets: a cut pile fabric made in silk, cotton and man-made fibres. (Dralon has become known as a velvet pile fabric, although it is, in fact, the name of a yarn, rather than a type of fabric. When Dralon is made into a velvet pile it can be sponged or dry-cleaned easily.)

Vynide: another leather-look, laminated fabric.

Weave: weaves belong to the 'tweed family' and are generally made in wool or cotton. They are now available with a latex backing and a man-made fibre surface. These fabrics make a very good imitation of tweed or weaves and they can be sponged clean without the water penetrating the stuffing underneath.

11 MEASURING AND ESTIMATING

To estimate the amount of fabric required for covering a piece of furniture the piece must be measured accurately, taking into account the pattern and weave of the fabric and the style of the piece of furniture. With a patterned fabric, the pattern on the arms should run round in line with the inside back and ensure, too, that the pattern is central on the inside back and that this lines up with the pattern on the seat, cushion and front border. When measuring fabric for a buttoned back piece, leave extra large seam allowances to ensure that there will be enough fabric to pull down into each button well (page 65). If the fabric has a pile, this must always run down on the piece of furniture. (After cutting mark the top of each piece with chalk to help you get the fabric the right way up.)

Take a sheet of paper, and write down all the different parts of the piece of furniture and their measurements. This becomes the 'cut' sheet (fig. 61). Measure each length in the direction shown (fig. 62) and using abbreviations write down the length first, then the width of each part of the item of furniture. Make a plan of the piece of fabric by drawing on paper the exact area and shape that each piece will take, roughly to scale. Use this as a guide when cutting the cover. When measuring, add at least 10 cm (4 in) on the tuck-in (the tuck-in is the flap of material which tucks in between the seat and the inside back) and at least 5 cm (2 in) extra on all other pieces. However, there is no need to allow enough margin to stretch to the actual place where it is tacked to the frame. Generally, an extra piece of hessian (called a fly) is sewn on, to make up this length. Flys are used to reduce bulk and also to save fabric. Up to 1 metre (1 yard) can be saved on a chair by using flys in the tuck in.

60 *Positioning patterns*

Chair sizes

	cm length × cm width	inch length × inch width
Inside back	76 × 65	27½ × 25½
Seat	65 × 85	25½ × 33½
Inside arms	52 × 75	20½ × 29½
Outside arms	40 × 80	16 × 32
Front border	25 × 55	10 × 21½
Front scrolls	40 × 18	16 × 7
Back scrolls	30 × 16	12 × 6
Outside back	76 × 56	30 × 22
Cushion	56 × 50	22 × 20
Cushion borders	10 × 56	4 × 22
Piping	50 × width	20 × width

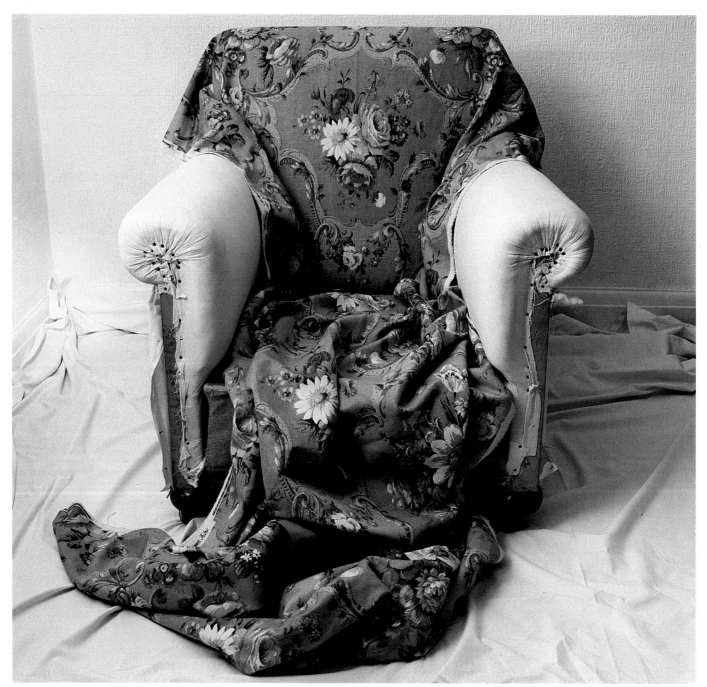

Positioning of patterned cover fabric

46

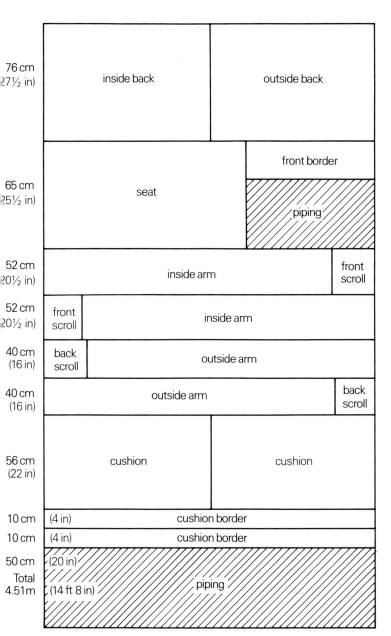

76 cm (27½ in) — inside back | outside back

65 cm (25½ in) — seat | front border | piping

52 cm (20½ in) — inside arm | front scroll

52 cm (20½ in) — front scroll | inside arm

40 cm (16 in) — back scroll | outside arm

40 cm (16 in) — outside arm | back scroll

56 cm (22 in) — cushion | cushion

10 cm (4 in) — cushion border

10 cm (4 in) — cushion border

50 cm (20 in) — piping

Total 4.51m (14 ft 8 in)

61 Cutting plan for easy chair

62 Four scroll easy chair

back scroll

inside back

front scroll

inside arm

inside arm

cushion

outside back

outside arm

cushion border

cushion

front border

   Check that you have allowed for all the pieces. Add the component lengths together to give the overall length of fabric needed for the chair cover. When estimating the length of piping remember that you will need to pipe the front scrolls and back scrolls, front borders, and the top and bottom edge of the seat cushion. Approximately 6.5 metres (6 yards) of piping can be made from 25 cm (10 in) of fabric if it is 122 cm (48½ in) wide.

12 PIPING AND RUCHING

CUTTING AND MAKING PIPING (WELTING)

Piping is used in both upholstery and soft furnishing. It is usually called 'welting' by upholsterers and 'piping' by soft furnishers. To cut and make a length of piping, lay the fabric flat on a table and fold one corner over until it forms a right angle. Cut along the fold, and then from the cut edge, measure strips 3.5 cm (1½ in) wide and cut into lengths. Join each length from corner to corner, with the right sides together to produce one long length. Trim the turnings to 1.25 cm (½ in) and open out flat.

Lay piping cord in the prepared length of piping, and fold over the fabric lengthwise. Using a grooved or a zip foot on the machine, sew along the length keeping the stitching close to the cord, without catching it in. The piping is now ready to stitch to the fabric/cover. Different gauge piping cord is available and the choice must depend on the thickness of the fabric to be welted, and the effect required. As a general principle, a thick fabric requires a thin cord and a fine fabric needs a thick cord. The most popular sizes are '00' and '4'. To join piping in a complete circle (for example, for a cushion top) the following method is used. Lay the two ends of the strip out flat; fold back in a straight line so that the

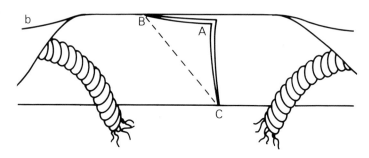

folds meet. Cut across each piece leaving 1.25 cm (½ in) turning from the fold. Take the top corner of one piece and place it to the lower corner of the opposite piece. A to A. Pin across diagonally B to C. Trim off to 13 mm (½ in) and open the seam out flat. Now place the two lengths of cord side by side and cut directly through the centre. The two ends of the cord will now butt together without leaving a gap. Fold the welt over the cord and continue the stitching line.

MAKING PIPING BY THE CYLINDER METHOD

This method is the most economical way of using small lengths of fabric; it can be used on any material including pile fabrics. First trim the fabric so that the sides are even. Then fold one corner at an angle of 30° across the width, so that it runs across the grain of the fabric. This allows the piping to stretch. Fold the diagonally opposite corner across the width at exactly the same degree. (To make sure that the angle is the same at both ends, measure from A to B and then make C to D the same length.) Pin corner C 4 cm (1½ in) from the edge of corner A. Join along this line until the other end is

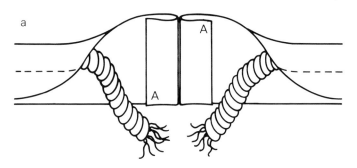

63 Above and right Joining lengths of piping

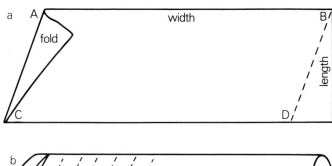

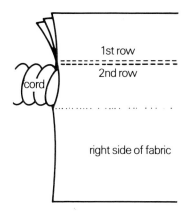

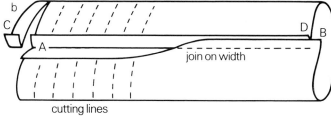

64 Making piping using the cylinder method

65 *Sew piping to first length of fabric*

reached. (At this stage, if the fabric is wide, the cylinder formed by the join may start to twist, this does not matter.) On reaching the opposite end you will find that corner B is 4 cm (1½ in) longer than corner D. Machine sew the join across using a small stitch and press open the seam. Start cutting from corner A in a continuous strip 4 cm (1½ in) wide. The strip is now ready to insert the piping cord.

JOINING PIPING TO THE MAIN FABRIC

Take the lengths of piping and join them together (page 48). With practice the cord can be placed in its outer case and straight on to the fabric. Beginners, however, are advised to make up the piping with the cord inserted before joining it to the fabric. It is most important that the cover is piped well, as wrinkled piping can spoil what might otherwise have been a very good piece of work. Machine stitch the piping to the right side of the first piece of fabric close to the seam line. Place the second piece of

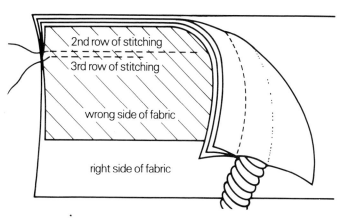

66 *Add second piece of fabric to complete piped seam*

fabric (right side against the piping) and stitch a second line. Turn the whole piece to the right side; the cord is now firmly inserted between the two lengths of fabric. If the last row of stitching was close enough to the cord, there should be no stitching visible on the right side.

When approaching a corner during piping, stitch up to the corner and make a cut into the edge of the fabric almost up to the needle. Now, leaving the needle in the corner of the welt, lift the presser foot, turn sharply at the corner, replace the foot and continue stitching. On a curve, snip the piping to help ease it into position.

APPLYING RUCHE (CUT OR UNCUT) TO THE MAIN FABRIC

Ruche can be bought by the metre with either cut or uncut edges. It is available in many colours and varies between 2 and 3 cm (¾ in and 1½ in) in depth. Ruche is joined to the main cover in exactly the same way as the piping welt. Make sure that the fluffy edge lies away from the edge and that the stitching is kept in a straight line. To join the ruche cut 1.25 cm (½ in) longer than the fabric, and lap one piece over the oher. Stitch across both, taking care to keep them in line. Turn the corner at a right angle by easing the ruche so that it is extra full at the corner. Unlike piping, ruche must not be cut on a corner or it will fray badly.

13 SPRUNG EASY CHAIR

The sprung easy chair takes a traditional style of covering and the process begins with the seat. Having cut out the seat fabric so that it stretches at least 6 cm (2½ in) into the tuck-in, cut flys for the outside back and for the two sides which will reach from the fabric to the base rail with a 5 cm (2 in) allowance for turning. (A fly is used on the seat and on the back of a chair in the tuck-in area. Use strong lining, hessian or odd pieces of fabric.) The fly must be folded back 1.25 cm (½ in) before being stitched to the cover so that the threads do not pull away when under pressure. Join the fly along the two sides and the back.

A sprung easy chair does not need a fly which comes right to the front of the cover because it has to be cut away around the chair upright. Nonetheless, you should use a piece of cover fabric for this fly as it is visible at the front edge. Centralize the seat cover on the chair and temporary tack the flys to the back and to the two side base rails. Smooth the cover forward and using skewers attach the seat firmly under the front lip. Smooth the seat out towards the sides, and after cutting round the uprights at the back and sides (fig 68), tack in place.

Stitch right through the cover into the hessian, using a

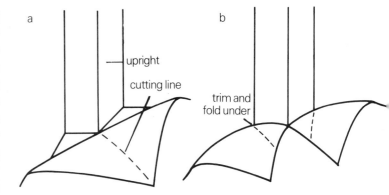

67 *Cutting round upright*

back stitch. Fold the corners under, making sure that they are symmetrical. Place the front border in position using skewers and fold under the top edge. Secure it so that the previous stitch line is covered. Place a length of sheet wadding on to the calico, and pull the cover over the top; temporary tack it to the underside of the base rail. If the front edge is sprung, make a snip just below the top front rail (fig. 68) and temporary tack the raw edge to the front facings on the lower part. Turn in the upper part and pin in line with the edge of the border.

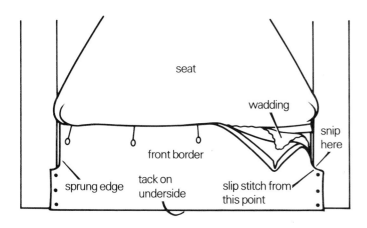

68 Covering front border

On the firm edge tack the raw edge of the front border on to the facing on both sides. Slip stitch along the top edge.

This type of border is corded, but as an alternative, a row of piping can be machined across the top of the front border before attaching it to the chair. The front is stitched on in the same manner, with the piping showing between the seat and border.

THE PLATFORM SEAT
Different styles of chairs obviously need different approaches to covering. A platform seat is unusual in that it has a separate seat cushion. Generally, the platform is covered with a platform cloth that matches the main fabric and the lip (about 15 cm/6 in deep) is covered in the main fabric.

With right sides together sew the front lip to the platform cloth leaving a 1.25 cm (½ in) seam allowance. Take a length of cotton webbing about 3 cm (1¼ in) wide and stitch it by machine to the back edge of the lip where it joins the platform cloth. Stitch right through the seam allowance starting and finishing off firmly. Stitch only the actual width taken up by the seat, not the tuck-in area. The webbing should, however, extend down into the tuck-in so that it may be secured to the frame.

Having sewn the webbing in place, pipe the front border from the point where it meets the scroll or outside arm (depending on the type of chair). Assemble the front border and the lip, and turn the 'right way out'. Place the front lip in position on the seat and check that it fits snugly round the front border. Pull the two lengths of webbing at either side of the lip, and temporary tack them to the bottom rail of the frame. Push the platform cloth in place, and secure with temporary tacks to the sides and back of the frame.

Turn the front border back to expose the webbing; then, using a curved needle and twine, sew right through the webbing, making sure the stitches catch right through to the stuffing.

Place a length of wadding over the lip and front border area of the chair, pull the fabric over the top of this, cutting around the frame upright. Tack in place underneath the frame, making sure that the seam allowances on the piping are turned flat, before tacking home. The chair is now ready for the next process.

THE MODERN SEAT
Covering the lip and front border on a modern chair which has tension springs or rubber webbing seat demands a slightly different approach. This type of seat usually has a platform cloth laid over the tension springs. The cloth can be padded by stitching it to a thin layer of foam or felt. Along the back of the platform cloth, stitch a tube wide enough for a tension spring to pass through. Now attach a piece of the main covering fabric to the front edge of the platform cloth, while at the same time and on the same line, sew to the underside a length of hessian wide enough to stretch over the front lip. Pull the platform cloth forward to the front border of the chair. Bring the hessian forward over the lip and front border,

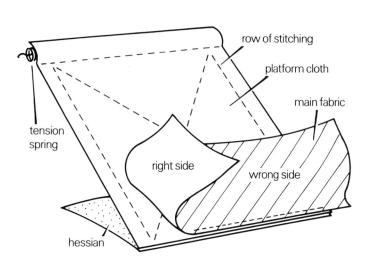

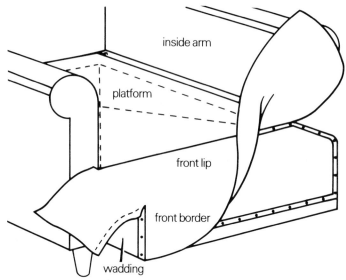

70 Fitting platform cloth

69 Attaching hessian and cover fabric to platform cloth

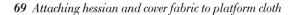

turn the edges under and tack to border frame.

Take a piece of 5 mm (¼ in) foam and fit it over the lip, front border, and down the sides of the front border. Over the foam, place a length of wadding to cover right to the bottom edge of the frame. Pull the main cover over the lip and border, and temporary tack under the frame on the front edge. Turn under the bottom edge of the corner, trimming off the excess fabric back to 1.25 cm (½ in). Turn under the upright edge towards the scroll. Tack the fabric under the frame at the base and then slipstitch the front corner, making a neat finish. Repeat this process on the other side of the chair.

In some cases, a fireside chair with a polished wooden frame will be sprung with tension springs or rubber webbing. The platform can be made in the same way as for the traditional chair, by padding and stitching a length of platform cloth. The size must allow for a slot to be made at both ends for a spring to be slotted through.

In the same way as for the traditional chair, the front edge has a piece of the main fabric stitched to the platform cloth so that the hessian is not visible. The depth of the main fabric should be approximately 20 cm (8 in) to allow for the turn under. Thread tension springs or rubber webbing through the slots, and attach these to the fittings on the sides of the frame.

INSIDE ARMS AND INSIDE BACK
The re-covering process described first is for a traditional chair. Re-covering the arms on a modern chair is slightly different (page 53). Place the fabric for the inside arm in position leaving enough overlap in the front to pleat on to the front facing. Temporary tack under the arm at the front, and, keeping the pattern or grain of the fabric horizontal, pull the cover towards the back and temporary tack in place (fig. 73). Push the cover through between the rails of the arm and seat and temporary tack to the base rail. When satisfied that the arm is in the correct position, cut round the front upright from the

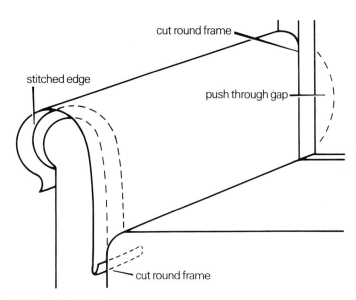

71 *Covering inside arm*

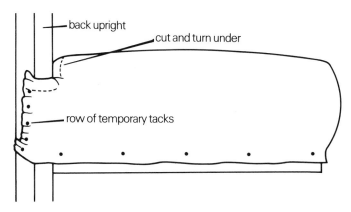

72 *Fitting cover fabric around upright*

point where it will not tuck away. Push the spring edge down to find this point. Trim back to 1.25 cm (½ in) and turn under. Pull the rest of the cover right through under the rail and temporary tack in place.

Cut the cover at the back rail, push through between the web and the rail leaving free at this stage. Cut the fabric into the frame at the top of the arm allowing the fabric to spread round to the back. Temporary tack to the back upright. Keep the fabric taut between the back and front and temporary tack to the rail. Using a strong twine fasten one end to a tack placed at the bottom of the facing and then run a row of stitches along the edge of the fabric, pull as you sew until they are tight. Place a temporary tack in the corner of the facing where the straight edge becomes curved, wind the twine around it and tack home. Even the gathers out round the scroll and tack in place using 13 mm (½ in) gimp pins keeping to the line of the scroll. Cut off the twine, and trim the edges back to the tack line. Leave the arms at this stage and start on the inside back.

Place the cover on the back keeping the pattern central. Hold it in place with skewers along the top of the outside back, push the cover through the lower back rail and position a temporary tack in the centre of the rail.

ARMS ON A MODERN CHAIR

Start re-covering the arms of a modern chair once the inside back has reached the stage described in the last section. On a modern chair, the inside and outside arms are piped and then sewn ready to use in one piece. The cover must be cut and pinned to fit the contour of the arm leaving extra length on the cloth to enable the cover to be pulled on. The excess is cut away after the cover has been tacked in place. Back up the outside arms and place wadding over inside and outside arm before placing on the sewn cover. The inside of the arm must be cut into the frame first. When this is all in place, tack home. Pull the outside arm into place and tack home on the underside of the frame and down the outside back upright.

Working on the inside back, now push the cover in at

the point where the inside arm and inside back meet. Mark this line with chalk and mark also the point where the frame joins at the base of the arms and back, as the fabric has to be cut away at this point to allow free passage round the frame. Trim the fabric back to within 1.25 cm (½ in) of the marking, and remove the cover from the chair.

Cut strips of the main fabric to use as a collar for the inside back. Then cut strips of hessian for flys to fit on the lower edge. The collar can be piped if the style of chair is a bordered back (characteristic of the sprung-back armchair), otherwise it is joined as a plain seam. The collar ensures a good fit and enables the fabric to spread out and follow the contour of the arms, thus preventing the fabric from splitting. Having stitched the flys in place and joined the collars to the back, place the fabric on the chair again lining up the pattern if any, with the seat. Secure at the bottom edge by temporary tacking into the base rail at a point in the centre of the fabric. Check that the layer of wadding is smooth, then tack the fabric to the back of the top rail, so that the cover is pulled over the top edge. Place a tack on either side of the upright rails, again pulling the fabric right through to the back.

Push the collars through the opening between the inside arm and inside back and after making sure that they are smoothly in position tack in place on to the uprights. The inside arms that were left untacked can now be pulled through and tacked in place on to the uprights.

By pushing the inside back cover with one hand and pulling with the other hand, smooth from the centres out towards the corners and temporary tack in place. Cut into the frame on the lower rail and, leaving a 2.5 cm (1 in) turning, fold under, round the frame. Pull down and tack in position. Fold the fly over so that the tacks are through the double fabric, this will prevent the fly from fraying out if any strain is put on it. Continue to

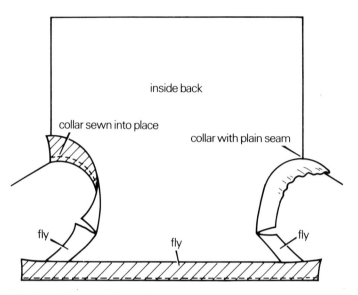

73 Sew collars and flys to inside back

tack all round until the top corners are reached. If the corner is square then smooth the fabric from along the back and up from the sides until it meets at the corner in a dart. Cut along this dart leaving 2.5 cm (1 in) to turn under. On a round corner two darts from front to back will be needed if the back is deep. On a shallow back, however, the fabric can be eased over the edge of the back without any pleats or darts on the front surface.

After the darts or pleats have been placed in original position, check that the pattern is still central, and that it is running round in line with the inside arms. When this has been checked, the tacks can be hammered home, and any excess fabric may be cut off. The next step is to place the outside pieces in position. On a firm back chair with padded arms, there is no need for a collar. Place the fabric on the chair and temporary tack in position on the bottom rail, on the top of the outside back and on the sides of the outside back. When the fabric is in position, start to push the fabric through the gap between the inside arms and inside back. The cover must be cut at the points at which its free passage is restricted by the frame.

At this stage back up the outside arms with hessian. Place a length of sheet wadding over this whole area, before applying the cover fabric.

OUTSIDE ARMS

On a traditional chair, the next step is to cover the outside arm. (This will already have been covered on a modern chair.) Starting with the outside arm, leave an allowance of at least 2.5 cm (1 in) proud of the front scroll at its widest point. Line the fabric up so that the pattern or grain of the fabric is running parallel with the floor and temporary tack to hold in place. Fold back the fabric where it meets the inside arm on the rail, mark along this line by folding with the thumb or marking with chalk.

Cut a length of back tacking strip (buckram or cardboard can be used) to the length of the arm less 1.25 cm (½ in) at each end. Lay the fabric back over the arm and line up the mark under the inside arm. Place the strip as hard against the inside arm as it will go and then tack along the strip making sure the line of the fabric remains in place. Trim off excess fabric and then place the sheet wadding so that it covers the tacks. Pull the fabric back down and secure under the base frame with a few temporary tacks. Secure the fabric on the front scroll and outside back in the same manner. Fill in with tacks and tack home.

SCROLLS

Cut out the scrolls to shape by taking a template on a piece of card. Follow the line of the frame on the outer edge and the line just inside the stitched edge on the inner edge.

Cut the fabric 1.25 cm (½ in) larger than the

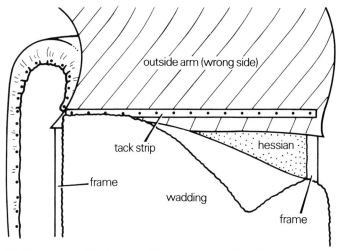

74 Fitting cover fabric to outside arm using back tack strip

template all round, keeping the pattern or grain lines upright. Turn the edges over the template and press down with your thumb, hard enough to make a crease line. Remove the template and place a layer of wadding in its place. Using skewers, place the padded scroll in place with the edges turned under. Temporary tack on the underside at the base of the frame and then slip stitch in position all round the scroll. This type of scroll would be corded to match the front border. Start and finish the cording on the underside of the base frame. However, if the front border is piped, the scroll may be piped before stitching in position on the chair.

If the scroll is finished right to the edge, proceed as follows. Pin the fabric in position on the inside arm, following the outer edge where it dips inwards under the outside arm. The fabric must be left with a 4 cm (1½ in) turning, while the remaining layers should be trimmed back to 1.25 cm (½ in), and notched to match the inside arm. Starting from the bottom, the piping can then be stitched around the facing up to the point at which it meets the outside arm. Leave a length of piping hanging from this point, sufficient to tack along the length of the outside arm.

Using the machine, join the facings to the inside arm, up to the underside of the arm. The arm is pulled over and fixed at this point, when this has been done. Pull the excess fabric at the side of the facing round to the outside arm and tack down. Tack the piping down the edge finishing just under the edge of the base frame. The outside arm is now back tacked in place and where it meets the front facing it is slip stitched, catching in the piping and the front facing. At the point where the front border meets the front facing, the piping must be tucked under and slip stitched over the front border.

On an overstuff scroll, the facing would be cut to the inner shape; allowing 1.25 cm (½ in) turning, it is then padded with wadding and fixed in position with skewers. It can be piped round the edges or corded. Slip stitch in place using a waxed thread and a cording needle (fig. 76).

Some types of facing are made from wood. With

these, the facing is padded with a layer of wadding after a fixing bolt has been placed through the wood. The fabric is then placed on the facing and pulled over the edges so that it can be stapled or glued to the wood. 5 mm (¼ in) tacks may be used if the wood is of sufficient thickness. Fit the facing into position on the front of the arm, and then finish the outside arm. This type of facing is usual on leather-covered chairs and can be finished with close nailing. Generally, it is best to follow the style of the original trimming, but depending on the fabric used, the appearance of a chair can be enhanced by the choice of a different type of trimming.

The outside back is the next section to be covered. Start by backing up with a length of hessian or calico in the same way as for the outside arms. Place a length of wadding to fit over this and back tack the outside back along the top edge of the frame keeping just below the frame line. Pull the fabric over the wadding, temporary tack on the underside of the base, turn in the sides, and slip stitch in place using a cording needle. Tack home the tacks in the base, and trim off the surplus fabric.

Turn the chair completely upside down and if the chair has castors fitted directly to the frame, lever them out from their sockets. Cut a length of 213 g (7½ oz) hessian or black linette to fit the base allowing an extra 1.5 cm (⅝ in) all round. Turn the fabric under and starting from the four centre points at the front, back and sides, tack 8 cm (3 in) just inside the frame edge. Work from the centres towards the legs.

Cut into the legs at a right angle, turn under and tack home (the tacks should be placed at intervals of approximately 3.5 cm [1½ in]). Now refit the castors. Starting directly above the centre of the castor socket, make a series of cuts in the hessian (or black linette) from the centre to the side of the socket. Turn under and tack down, then replace the castor.

Turn the chair the right way up, check that all the

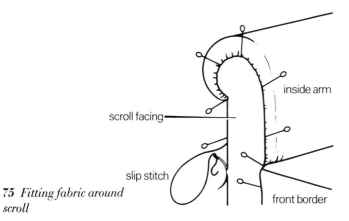

75 *Fitting fabric around scroll*

inside arm

scroll facing

slip stitch

front border

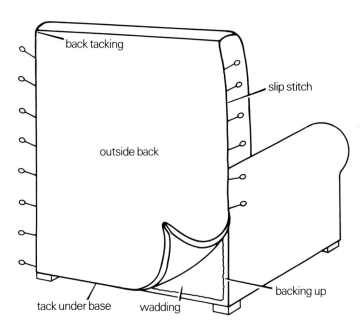

76 *Covering outside back*

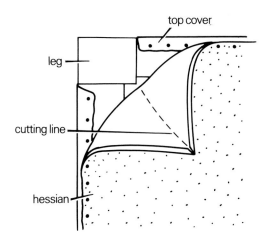

77 *Fitting hessian around leg*

threads have been cut off and finished tidily. Brush off any surplus fluff or dust using a pad made of the same fabric. If it is a pile cloth, finish by brushing the pile down towards the ground. A fringe can be sewn on at this stage if required (page 73), in every other respect the chair is ready for use.

FLUTING

Fluting is sometimes worked on the inside back of a chair. It has an attractive effect and adds extra padding. To make up a piece of fluting, cut a length of hessian to fit the back with an extra allowance of 20 cm (8 in) all round to allow for take-up. Starting in the centre draw a vertical line. Then mark off more vertical lines down the fabric at intervals of 10 cm (4 in). This width can be varied according to taste. Mark the main fabric in the same way on the wrong side allowing an extra 5 cm (2 in) for each strip to allow for padding and stitching.

In a factory or large workshop, the padding would be pre-covered in long lengths which could be slid into place with a tool. The padding is usually linter felt which is liable to break up if it is pushed into a tube and result in a lumpy mess. Nowadays, as fluting is a 'one-off', I suggest using the following method. Start on the left-hand side with the hessian laying flat. Crease down all

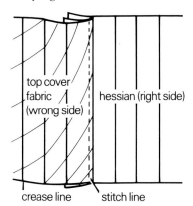

78 *Fluting with crease lines*

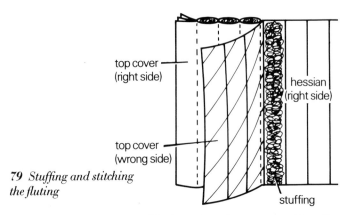

top cover
(right side)

hessian
(right side)

top cover
(wrong side)

stuffing

79 *Stuffing and stitching
the fluting*

High back chair

the lines on the main fabric using the wrong side of a
ruler. Lay the first crease on the first mark on the
hessian, and fold back, taking a small turning approxi-
ately 1.25 cm (½ in) stitch line from top to bottom (fig.
79). Take a length of linter felt and lay it on the hessian
(use enough linter felt to fill the pad out tight). Then
stitch the fabric down the crease line on to the hessian in
the same manner as the first line (fig. 80). Continue
across until all lines are sewn and padded. The fluting is
now ready to use as a normal length of fabric to re-cover
the chair back or seat as the case may be. Pad the outside
flutes before tacking home.

14 WINGS

There are many different types of wings and methods of covering them differ accordingly. However, this basic method of covering used for an overstuff wing with a stitched edge, can be adapted to suit most traditional types. Place a length of wadding over the wing, trimming back to the edge by tearing with the fingers. The piece of fabric already cut should measure from the widest points both ways with an allowance of 5 cm (2 in) extra on each measurement. Place the fabric for the inside wing with the grain running vertically, and secure with a few temporary tacks to hold it in place. Push the excess fabric through the space between the frame, two cuts must be made to accommodate the frame. Cut right to the frame, so that the fabric will spread round towards the outside back. Trim back to within 1.25 mm (½ in) of the cuts and turn the fabric under. Temporary tack over the back edge.

Push the fabric down to meet the inside arm and make a cut, to allow the fabric to spread. Trim back to 1.25 cm (½ in) and fold under. Secure with skewers ready to be slip stitched. Ease the fabric round the outside of the wing, making two pleats where the excess fabric meets at the widest part of the curve. Tack round the outside wing approximately 3 cm (1¼ in) from the edge. Pull the fabric, calico and hessian through to the back upright and tack in place. Slip stitch round the lower edge of the wing.

Now 'back up' the outside wing with a length of hessian. Tack the hessian over the hollow section attaching it to the frame below the part where the fabric has already been tacked. Cover the whole outside wing area with wadding, trimming it off at the outer edge. Place a length of fabric over the wing and trim to shape, allowing a 2 cm (¾ in) turn under all round. Tack the fabric in place along the back edge on the outside back. Turn under the edges on the remainder of the fabric, fix with skewers just shy of the edge and slip stitch in place. Leave the lower edge free to tuck under the inside arm.

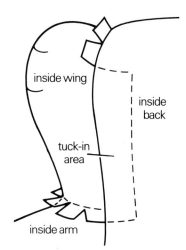

80 Covering inside wing

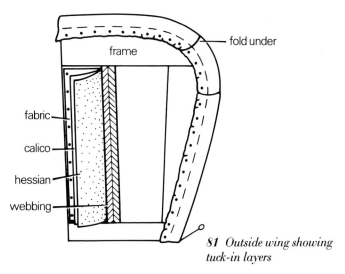

81 Outside wing showing tuck-in layers

The wing may have a piping between the inside and outside wing. This should be tacked on after the inside wings have been finished and before the outside wings have been started. It starts at the lower edge of the wing, goes round the outside wing, across the outside back and finishes at the base of the opposite wing. The outsides are then skewered in place and slip stitched catching the piping and securing it in place between the inner and outer wings.

RE-COVERING A MODERN WING CHAIR

Modern chairs often have flat wings which means that the inside wing and the outside wing can be joined before fitting. Trim down to allow 1.25 mm (½ in) turn under then machine together. Piping can be inserted at this stage if required. (Cut notches in the seam allowance so that they may be matched with machining to prevent any twisting.) Now, lay padding (linter felt or foam) on to the wing of the chair and fit the wing covering. Pull the complete wing on over the padding and cut the inside wing in exactly the same way as before (page 59). Tack in place. Pull the outside wing towards the outside back and secure to the upright. Leave the bottom edge of the wing free, so that the outside arm will cover the raw edge. This bottom edge will be secured when the outside arm is back tacked in place.

15 CUSHIONS

CUTTING AND MAKING A DOWN OR FEATHER CUSHION PAD

Use a fabric called downproof cambric for these cushion pads. Make sure the seams are waxed after sewing, to prevent the down penetrating them. Use a piece of beeswax to rub along the sewing line. (A second row of stitching on the edge of the turning is an extra safeguard.) To make a flat cushion pad, measure the downproof cambric to the size you require the cushion to be. Cut two pieces leaving seam allowances of 1.25 cm (½ in) each side, then add an extra 2 cm (¾ in) all round. Lay out the two pieces with right sides together and machine round the edge, leaving the 1.25 cm (½ in) seam allowance. Start machining all round leaving a gap large enough to allow the case to be filled (about half the length of one side).

Make a second row of stitching along the outer edge and wax the stitching lines. Turn the cover right side out and fill with down or feathers. Turn the edges of the opening inside and top stitch along the edge. Wax the stitches. A good guideline when filling a cushion is to ensure that the corners are well filled and that the centre is convex in shape. When pressed in the middle, the pad should feel spongy; if it resists light pressure, it is overfilled.

CUTTING AND MAKING A BORDERED CUSHION WITH PARTITIONS

The advantage of adding inner walls to a bordered cushion is that the filling remains evenly distributed. Measure the cushion pad to be covered along the length, width and border depth. Add 2.5 cm (1 in) to each measurement for seam allowance. Then add an extra 2.5 cm (1 in) all round and cut. (Cut the border length in two pieces.) In addition, cut an extra border length to use as partition walls.

After cutting, lay the top and underside of the cushion with wrong sides up and mark with a pencil two lines

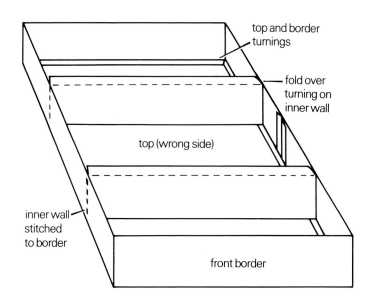

82 *Bordered cushion pad showing inner walls*

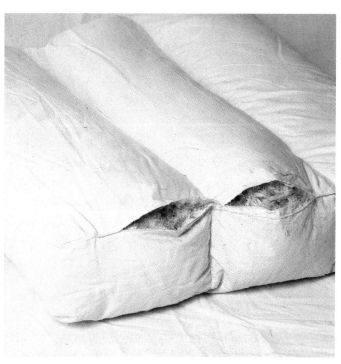

Bordered cushion showing down stuffing

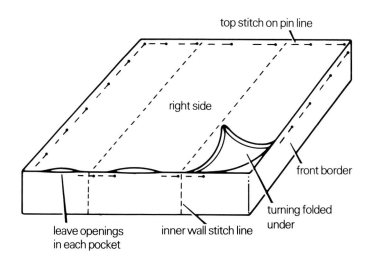

83 *Stitching underside of cushion to inner walls*

across the width, dividing each piece of fabric into thirds. Machine sew together and mark the two side borders to line up with the marks on the cushion. Cut the extra length of border into walls to fit the size of the cushion width. Fold over the 1.5 cm (⅝ in) seam allowance on the partition walls. Stitch the walls to the wrong side of the top side of the cushion, leaving the seam allowances unstitched. With right sides together, join the border to the top section. Take care not to catch the partition walls at this stage. Turn right side out. Stitch the partition walls upright to the side borders along the markings. Stop the stitching at the seam allowance. Fold over the seam allowance.

Place the underside fabric flat and match the inner walls to the pencil marks across the width. Stitch across, starting at the front, or first, inner wall, to prevent the seam allowance being inaccessible. After stitching the walls in place, the border edges and underside edges must be turned in and joined. Pin the two edges together all the way round the cushion leaving a gap in each section so that they can be filled with down.

Fill the individual sections, and test to see if they are evenly filled. First check that the corners are well filled and that the centre of each section is slightly convex. When pressed in the middle, the pad should feel spongy; if it resists light pressure, it is overfilled. After filling, fold in the edges of each gap and continue the top stitch to close the cushion.

CUTTING AND MAKING A BORDERED CUSHION WITHOUT PARTITIONS

Measure the cushion to be covered and cut out the pieces as described on page 60 (leaving out the extra fabric required for partition walls). When cutting a seat or back cushion, make sure that the pattern runs in line with the back and front border.

Cut out all the pieces before attempting to assemble the cushion. With right sides together, lay the centre of one piece of border against the centre front on the top side. Check that the pattern on the border runs down in line with the top side of the cushion. Pin the two border pieces round the cushion. Join together the ends of the border and, leaving a seam allowance, cut off any surplus. Cut a notch in the centre of the back and border seam. Unpin the border and flatten the seams on the side joins.

Make up a length of piping, and, starting at the notch at the back of the top side, pipe the top all round joining the piping when it meets at the back. Repeat on the underside of the cushion.

Before assembling decide how much opening to leave unstitched. For a down or foam cushion, leave the length

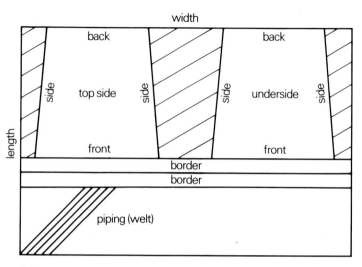

84 *Cutting plan for bordered seat cushion*

of the back of the cushion on the underside, but for a firm cushion it will be necessary to leave the cushion open halfway down each side as well as across the back of the underside. Starting at the notch, assemble the cushion by laying the top side on to the border (with right sides together), and stitching closer to the piping than previously. After stitching the two together, place the underside in position on the border, and line the corners up so that they are upright. Cut a notch in the seam allowance of each corner. Match up these notches as the cushion is stitched to prevent the cushion border being twisted on the finished article.

Make a second line of stitching nearer the piping on the part which is to be left open. This will keep the piping at an even thickness. Turn the cover right side out, fold the cushion pad in half, and push the front right into the corners. Turn the piping down towards the border as the pad is fitted in, to encourage the piping to stand up and make a good straight line.

With foam cushions, the front edge should be secured to stop the pad rolling round inside. Take two strips of

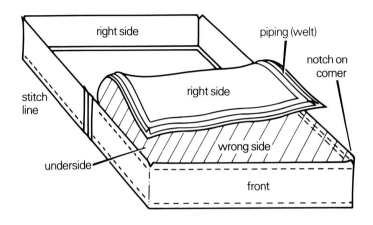

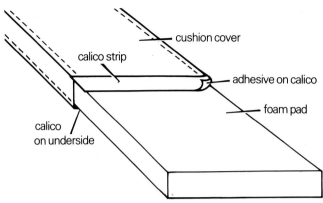

85 Cushion assembled with opening on underside

87 Fitting foam pad into cover

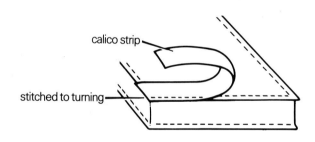

86 Attaching calico strip

calico, approximately 8 cm (3 in) wide and long enough to fit the cushion front. Machine the two strips on to the seam allowances on the front top side and front underside of the cushion cover. When the two strips have been stitched in place, spread adhesive on to both the strip and foam interior. (There are many adhesives on the market these days, each with a special purpose. Read the intructions to make sure the type being used is the right one for the purpose.) Stick the calico strips to the foam, making sure the foam is pushed right up against the front border. When the adhesive is dry, push the

foam pad into the cover as you turn the cover right side out. To close the cover, pin the opening together, fold in the raw edges and slip stitch with a linen thread or twine.

CUTTING AND MAKING A GATHERED CORNER CUSHION

A gathered corner cushion can be used as a back cushion, instead of the bordered type. Although it is piped as a flat cushion it does retain the depth on the corners, which makes it as thick as a bordered cushion.

To cut out, measure the inside pad, and add 1.25 cm (½ in) turning each side. Cut the top of the cushion, making sure that the pattern is central (if the fabric is plain, cut to the thread). At this stage cut a square shape only. Cut the underside of the cushion in exactly the same way as the top, matching the pattern so that the cushions may be reversed individually. When both pieces have been cut, with the wrong sides together, lay them flat on the table. Measure 8 cm (3 in) in from each corner, and strike a line across to each mark. This measurement will be approximately 10 cm (4 in). Repeat

63

this process at each corner, and then cut across each line.

The measurement given is for an average thickness cushion of 8 cm (3 in). For a deeper one, increase the measurement, so that the corner is cut out wider. Do *not* cut too much away as the more that is cut from the corner, the smaller the circumference of the cushion will be. The corner should now be pleated and pinned in position, either with four pleats or two, this is a matter of choice. Make sure the pleats face in towards each other, on the right side of the cushion (see fig. 88).

The measurement across the corner should now be 3 cm (1¼ in). This is the turning allowance and it applies whatever the measurement cut across the corner. It must be pleated in so that the pleats meet in the centre. Leave the pins in position, and continue to pleat the remaining corners on the top and the underside of the cushion. Now make up the piping and apply it to the cushion top, starting on the lower edge, halfway along.

Pipe the cushion as shown in fig. 85. When you reach the corner, make sure the pleats are lying flat and do not get caught up underneath. Follow the line of the outer edge of the fabric, taking care to leave the correct seam allowance (1.25 cm [½ in]). The stitching line should be slightly rounded at the corners. Join the ends of the

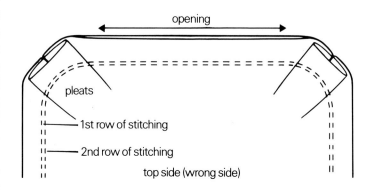

88 Inside of gathered corner cushion

piping together and, placing the right sides together, assemble the cushion. Leave a gap in the lower edge of the cover large enough for the cushion pad to be inserted. Before stitching the cushion together, sew an extra line close to the piping along the gap (page 62). This makes sure that the piping is the same thickness all round.

Fold the cushion pad in half and push it through the opening into the cover. Push the pad well into the corners and turn in the raw edges. Slip stitch the opening together with a linen thread.

16 HEADBOARDS

DEEP-BUTTON-BACKED HEADBOARD

To estimate the length of fabric you will need to cover the headboard, measure the widest part of the board, allow 10 cm (4 in) extra each side to turn round the back, and then add 5 cm (2 in) for every diamond. This total will constitute the width required. Measure the length in the same manner but exclude the unmarked base as this is covered separately.

Cut out the piece of fabric, leaving it square (do not trim it to shape). Mark the centre of the fabric with a cross (to find this use the method on page 38). The diamonds must be marked larger than they are on the board. On a board where the buttons are marked at 15 cm (6 in) intervals an extra 3 cm (1¼ in) will generally be sufficient. If, however, the board has been marked with different sized diamonds, place a piece of foam on the board between two measured button marks and, using a tape, measure over the foam from mark to mark. This will give the exact width required on fabric, for that diamond.

Mark the fabric on its wrong side in the same way as for the board, but using the new measurement. If you are using a pile fabric, the pile must run downwards, so mark the top. If the fabric is not wide enough to cover the entire width of the board, then it must be joined and this is called van dykeing. The seam follows the line of the pleats so that it is invisible when buttoned.

Van dykeing

To van dyke, machine stitch the two pieces together allowing one length to overlap the other by at least the width of half a diamond. Mark the whole piece of extra fabric with the button positions, keeping the marks in line. Pin the pleating lines right through the two pieces of fabric, then with a piece of chalk mark a curved line

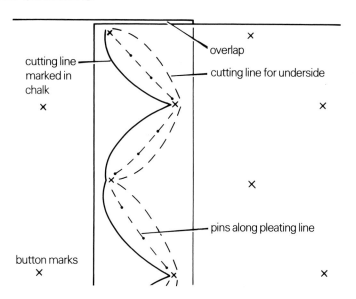

89 *Marking cutting line for van dykeing*

from the button mark to the button mark below, the widest part of the curve being about 2 cm (¾ in) graduating to about 3 mm (⅛ in) from the button mark.

After cutting the top piece of fabric turn the whole thing over and cut the underside as marked in fig. 90. Turn the pieces so that the two right sides are now together and place a pin through the two pieces right on the button mark. The outer curve of one side fits to the inner curve on the other side. Pin in place and machine stitch fairly close to the edge. Machine the two pieces together, stitching right to the button mark. Snip through the turning right to the button mark. This stitching must be accurate otherwise the pleating line will not be straight, if it is not cut in far enough at the buttons the pleat line will drag. Turn right side out. The piece of fabric is now ready to be used for buttoning.

Place a sheet of wadding, skin side up, on the foam,

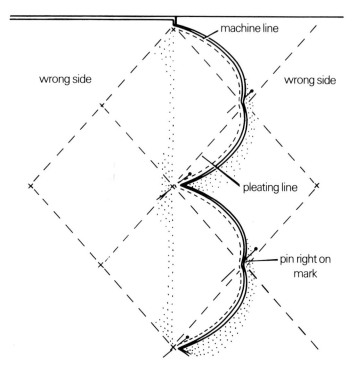

90 *Cutting fabric for van dykeing*

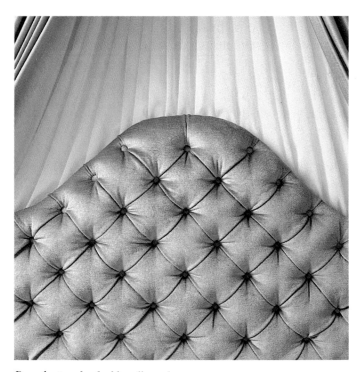

Deep-button-backed headboard

extending it well over the edges. Place the fabric over the wadding and cut lengths of button twine approximately 30 cm (12 in) long and put to the side. Take a long mattress needle (unthreaded) and push it eye first through the drilled centre mark on the back of the board. Take the fabric in one hand and find the centre button mark; push the needle through right on the mark far enough to allow you to thread the eye with a length of twine. Thread one end of the twine through the eye, thread the button on and then thread the remaining end of twine back through the eye. Pull through to the back. Place a tack just to the side of the hole on the back of the headboard. Wind one end of the twine round it and then hammer home. Place a second tack half-way in to the

board and pull the other end of the twine taut, at the same time push the button from the right side until it reaches the board, to take some of the strain. When the button is right home, wind the end of the twine round the tack and tack home. Repeat this until all the buttons are in place. Work away from the centre completing each diamond as you work. Use the flat end of the regulator to turn the pleats so that they are facing down.

When all the buttoning has been completed, pull the excess fabric round to the back of the board. Reduce the fullness by pleating the fabric and secure with temporary tacks at the back. The pleats do not always run off in line with the button work, particularly if the edges are shaped. Try to clean out any curves and then pleat the excess that forms into downward facing folds, making these balance on each side of the headboard. When you have arranged the pleats to your satisfaction, tack down the fabric on the back of the board and trim it back to the tack line.

When the back has been tacked in place, begin work on the bottom edge of the headboard. The foam should be cut with a sharp knife from each of the buttons on the bottom row down to the bottom edge. The fabric is then pulled tight so that it falls into the cut and thus forms a straight pleat. Tack the fabric home just below the marked line on the board. To finish this part of the board, cut a length of fabric to cover the remaining area on the board. Cut it wide enough to allow you to turn it round to the back and deep enough to go under the bottom edge to be tacked to the back. (Generally, about 10 cm [4 in] extra on all sides is sufficient.) If the fabric has to be joined to make up the width, make two joins each side of the central width. Using a length of buckram or webbing, back tack the fabric along the bottom pleats in a straight line (page 36). Place a length of wadding over the board, pull the fabric over and tack to the back of the board. Trim excess fabric up to the tack line.

Use a length of lining fabric to cover the back. Cut it to size, allowing 5 cm (2 in) extra all round for turning under. But first, lay a length of wadding on the board tearing it to shape using your fingers. Lay the lining on top and, using skewers, pin it in place. Slip stitch all round the edge. Alternatively, you could tack or staple the lining to the back of the headboard. Now the headboard is ready to be fitted either with screws, if it is to be attached to the wall, or with legs, if it is to be fitted to the back of a divan base. When you make the screw holes, use a bradawl to pierce the lining fabric before screwing in, otherwise the screw turns the fabric and tears it. Turn to the front and, using the flat end of the regulator to tuck under the folds, straighten all the pleats.

Float buttoning

Float buttoning is used on headboards, chairs and cushions. It is not only decorative but also useful for keeping the stuffing in place. The buttons are not pulled right down tight to the backing, instead, they are allowed to 'float', making only a shallow indentation on the front surface.

When float buttoning, the actual buttoning is done after the front fabric is backed in place, and no allowance is made for pleating. The twine should be tightened only enough to hold the button firmly in place; the degree of indentation is a matter of choice. The twine will be pulled through to the back and, depending on the type of backing, will either be tacked home or tied round a washer.

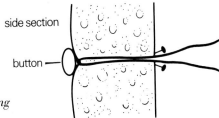

side section

button —

91 *Side section showing float button*

A cushion is sometimes float buttoned both sides. To do this, instead of fastening the twine around a tack or washer, you secure it to another button. Tie the button on, make a slip knot and pull the two buttons towards each other. Lock the knot and cut off the ends of twine.

MAKING A BORDER-EDGED HEADBOARD

This type of headboard can be made using foam for the centre pad, and linter felt for the outer edge. (See deep-button-backed headboard on page 38.) Cut the piece of board to shape, and then mark a line 10 cm (4 in) in from the edge, round the top and both sides. Draw another line 15 cm (6 in) up from the bottom edge;

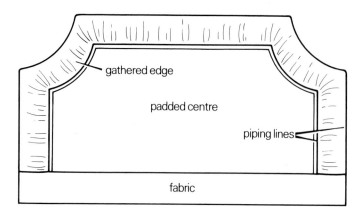

92 *Finished board showing gathered edge*

below this line the board is only slightly padded as this part goes behind the bed base and mattress. Cut a length of 5 cm (2 in) foam to fit the space between the lines. Add 3 cm (1¼ in) all round (see deep-button-backed headboard on page 38).

Chamfer the edge and stick strips of calico on the edges (fig. 53). Using staples or 10 mm (⅜ in) tacks, fix the edge of the foam directly to the marked line all round. Cover the foam with a layer of wadding, then place a length of fabric over the foam covered area, overlapping by approximately 1.25 cm (½ in). Tack or staple the fabric to the line marked all round. Trim away excess fabric and calico strips. Make up a length of piping (in the same or contrasting colour fabric), to go down the two sides and along the top edge twice. Now tack the piping to the board with the raw edges facing towards the outside edge. The piping should follow a line right round the edge of the foam, except for the bottom edge. When the piping reaches the corner, make a snip to prevent puckering.

Once the piping has been tacked in place the next step is the gathered edge. Measure the area to be covered on the outside edge of the board and double the measure-

ment; this should give you sufficient fullness in the gathers. Cut strips of fabric (across the width of the fabric) so that the pattern will be upright along the top to match the centre pad. The width of each strip should be 15 cm (6 in), this will allow room for the turnings and the padding. Now, machine the strips together to make one long length. Make a mark half-way along and at each quarter. Mark the board in the same way on both the inner and outer edge. This helps by providing a guideline to the amount of gathering required in each quarter and the marks also help keep the gathers upright along the top and horizontal on the sides. Put a line of 1.25 cm (½ in) stitches along the edges of the fabric strip. Using a strong thread, stop and start again at each

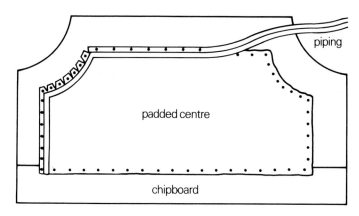

93 *Fixing piping around padded centre*

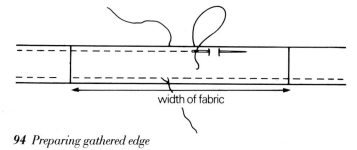

94 *Preparing gathered edge*

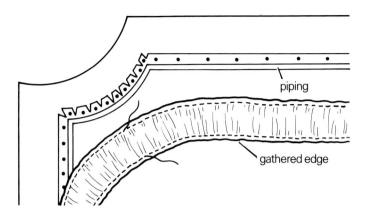

95 *Placing gathered edge around padded centre*

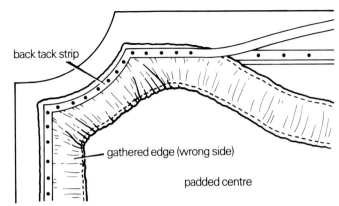

96 *Tacking on gathered edge using back tack strip*

quarter mark. Gather both edges so that the outer edge fits the board, then start on the first section on the side of the board. Lay the gathered strip right side down against the piped edge. Use a length of back tack strip or a strip of buckram tack close to the piped edge so that the gathers are caught against the piping. When you reach the corner of the inner edge, the gathers must be tacked closer together. This allows enough gathering to cover the extra length of the outer edge. Without this allowance, you will find that you have a flat area without gathers when you fit the outer edge.

Continue all round the board, finishing just below the line marked at the base. Once the inner part has been tacked home, place a length of linter felt on the unpadded edge of the board. (Polyester can be used instead of linter felt if you wish; in fact, if the fabric is light in colour polyester would be better.) Pad the edge so that it has a rounded appearance. Pull the gathered fabric over the padding and then temporary tack over the back edge.

When all the gathers are in position, tack home. Now, take the other length of piping and tack it all around the back edge of the board, starting at the base line. Keep the piping level, allowing it to stand just proud of the edge all

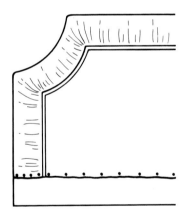

97 *Completed headboard*

round. Once the piping is complete, the next step is to pad the lower edge (page 67). Finally, finish the outside back in the same way as for the buttoned headboard (page 67).

Variations to a headboard can be made by deep buttoning or float buttoning the centre section. The suitability of these techniques will depend principally on the kind of fabric being used.

17 DEEP-BUTTON-BACKED CHAIR

Once the chair has been upholstered 'up to calico' or, alternatively, once it has had its outer cover removed, it is ready for re-covering.

First, using a cut sheet (page 45), cut out all the lengths of fabric required. Remember to allow for the extra taken up in buttoning (page 65). Mark all the pieces on the back with chalk for identification. The buttons should be made professionally; your local upholsterer or sewing shop will probably be able to do this. A 1.25 cm (½ in) button needs approximately 4 cm (1½ in) square of fabric. The metal shank buttons are widely used as they are stronger than the fabric-backed button.

I prefer to cover the seat of the chair first but it is a matter of choice. Place the cover square on the seat after positioning a sheet of wadding over the calico. Fix three temporary tacks in the back rail, pull the cover forward, and place three tacks in the underside of the rail at the front. Repeat from side to side, pushing the cover down between the back and seat rails. The cover will have to be cut round the uprights at this stage to allow the fabric to pass freely. Make sure the cover is placed correctly before cutting in to the uprights.

Pull the cover through between the seat and inside back and temporary tack it down on to the back rail. Smooth the cover forward and tack under the front rail. As the front of a seat has rounded corners, the excess fabric will have to be eased in along the bottom edge of the front. This can be done in two ways, either by bringing two pleats together at the centre of the leg, or by gathering a series of small pleats at the top of the chair leg.

If the leg is set back from the front of the frame, then tack the fabric right underneath. If it is level with the front then the fabric is tacked on to the face as low as

possible and later cut away flush and covered with gimp. Once the front is finished, tack home all round the back and sides and trim off any excess fabric.

Now place the correct piece of fabric square on the arm, leaving enough turnings all round. Place a button in the centre of the arm, going right through the fabric in the same manner as for the back (page 71). Tighten sufficiently to hold the fabric in place. Smooth the fabric up over the arm and secure with skewers underneath the stitched edge. Allow the fabric to form a pleat in a vertical line with the button, over the arm. Fix with a skewer and let the pleat continue from the button down into the tuck-in. Secure with a temporary tack to the base rail. Cut round the uprights and push the remainder of the fabric down through the tuck-in, temporary tack in place.

To finish around the front of the arm, wrap the fabric round the front forming pleats with the excess (face the pleats down towards the seat). Fix in place with skewers. Tighten up the button, tack home the tacks, snip the fabric round the curve where the inside back and arm meet so that it lies flat and then proceed to sew the cover to the underside of the arm right through the hessian (figs. 98–99).

The next stage is to mark up the fabric ready for buttoning the back. Measure and draw a vertical line down the centre of the fabric (because the fabric now has to stretch over the stuffing an extra allowance must be made to accommodate this). When measuring this, use a tape measure and push it right to the back hessian over the stuffing and to the nearest marked button on the hessian. This will give you the allowance needed. An average chair will need 2.5 cm (1 in) extra on the vertical and 2 cm (¾ in) on the horizontal. Mark out the measurements on the back of the fabric with a small cross at each button spacing. The markings are only used as a guide. A good deal depends on the way the fabric handles (i.e., if it stretches or folds well) and also on the fact that the lower buttons may be moved further away to allow for the curve. Most upholsterers 'feel' the buttons in, which is a skill learned by experience. Most beginners would be well advised to take a great deal of trouble in marking out as accurately as possible. If the chair has only to be re-covered, you can use the old cover as a guideline. Do not, however, cut a pattern from the old cover, as it will be much too small without the chair allowances left for stitching. It is very much better to re-cut a new cover to fit the chair rather than to try to make a chair fit a cover.

Once the fabric is marked out, cut a length of buttoning twine approximately 45 cm (18 in) long. Using a 25 cm (10 in) double-pointed needle, start to button the back. I prefer to tie off at the back of the chair, but if you prefer to tie off at the front then just reverse the following process, it will give the same result.

Starting with the mark nearest the centre, and working from the outside back, push the eye of the needle through the mark right to where the hair and wadding is parted. Find the corresponding mark on the piece of fabric and push the needle through from the wrong side. Thread the button on the twine and then thread both ends of twine through the eye of the needle. Pull the needle back through the chair, and tie an upholsterers slip knot in the twine. Roll up a small length of calico approximately 5 cm (2 in) wide until it makes a tube, and use this as a washer. Place the washer in between the back hessian and the knot, then pull the knot up until it grips the washer. Do not tighten up fully at this stage as the pleats formed in the front have to be manipulated into position. Working in this manner, form one diamond at a time. The excess material between the buttons should be folded under so that each pleat formed

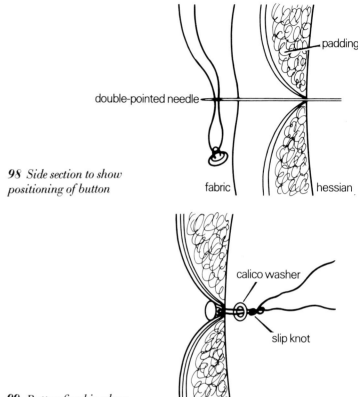

98 *Side section to show positioning of button*

99 *Button fixed in place*

is facing downwards. (This stops dust settling and also follows the way of the pile if this type of fabric is used.)

Using the spade end of the regulator, tuck the excess fabric under between each button keeping the fabric fairly taut between two buttons. The buttons will, of course, tighten down when the knots are tightened at the back of the hessian. Keep the padding even underneath each pad that is formed between the buttons and add more hair if necessary underneath the wadding. Continue to place all the buttons, and when they are even and the folds are all lying flat, tighten up the knots at the back. Check once more that they are even and fasten off by locking each slip knot with a single knot.

Fold the excess fabric into pleats, starting from the centre back and working towards the seat. Try to get each side balanced by manipulating the folds. When they are correct, skewer them in place on the underside of the top rail and sew all round. Overlap the inside back over the inside arm, snip to accommodate the curve and turn back under to make a fold. Place a button in position right on the fold line. The cover is now ready to be sewn all round (fig. 100).

Having sewn all round the outer part of the chair, break off a length of linter felt sufficient to cover the outside back and arm area, trim to shape with the fingers

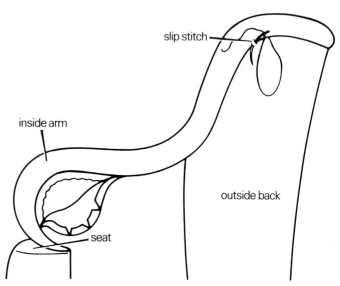

101 Fitting outside cover

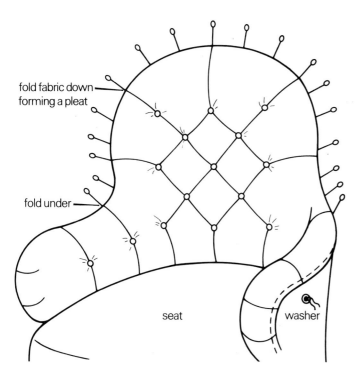

100 Arranging folds in fabric

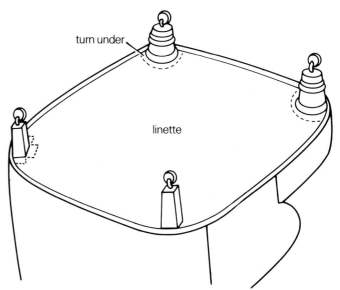

102 Fitting linette around legs

and place it on the outside back. Make sure it covers the stitch line. Take the outside arm fabric and place in position, trim back to shape leaving approximately 2 cm (¾ in) turnings. Turn this allowance under and skewer the cover in place, just under the edge of the rail. Pull the cover down and attach it under the wooden base rail, tacking at intervals of 4 cm (1½ in). Stitch the outside arm in place, using slipping thread and a slip stitch. Repeat the process to fit on the outside back. At the point at which the back meets the outside arm, trim away excess fabric and turn under; slip stitch in place (fig. 101).

Turn the chair upside down, to finish the underneath. Tack home all temporary tacks on the underneath of the frame. Cut a length of black linette to fit the base of the chair, turn the edge under and tack it to the bottom of the frame, thus covering all the raw edges. Cut round the legs to obtain a tidy fit, turn under the raw edge and tack home (fig. 102). If extra width is needed across the inside back (of a settee, for example) the fabric can be van dyked (page 65). However, if the piece has a curved back, it is not necessary to make the join by machine sewing. Instead, overlap on the folds leaving the raw edges tucked out of sight.

18 TRIMMINGS AND FINISHES

Chairs do not necessarily need trimming, but most chairs upholstered in the traditional manner come from an era when trimming was popular. Piping and ruche is applied during the re-covering process, but the trimmings and finishes which follow are all applied when re-covering is complete.

GIMP
Gimp is a type of braid that is used to conceal tacks at the edge of a show wood chair. It is usually .75 cm to 1.50 cm (⅜ to ⅝ in) wide, and is available in a number of designs and colours. To fix gimp, either use gimp pins which match the gimp in colour, or glue it using a good quality adhesive. If an adhesive is used, make sure it is designed for fabric before purchasing it. Scroll gimp is usually fixed with gimp pins as it has an uneven edge.

FRINGE
Fringe is usually applied at the base of a chair or as extra decoration along arms. It is best sewn on as this makes it stronger, although it is sometimes glued on in the same manner as the gimp. Most fringes used for trimming bases have a heading above the fringe, and this is the part that is sewn. The fringe should be positioned so that it hangs just clear of the carpet.

BRAIDING
Braiding is used to outline shape on inside backs, headboards, etc. Braid is usually wider and flatter than gimp and comes in a variety of designs. Mark the section to be braided with chalk and pin the braid in place. In an area which takes a good deal of wear, it is best machined in place on the fabric before re-covering. If, however, the area will receive light treatment, the braid can be hand-stitched in place after the article has been covered.

CORDING
Cording is generally used to cover a seam or to outline pleats, and can often be found on the chair edges and around scrolls. Cord usually consists of three lengths of silk-covered cord, twisted to form a rope. The ends will unravel easily so before cutting always bind the ends.

CLOSE NAILING

Close nailing is an effective type of finish, particularly on hide chairs. Antique nails are generally used and they can be bought in different finishes and diameters. The chair is covered and trimmed right to the rebate or the finished edge, and then the nails are hammered in place in an absolutely accurate line. When hammering in the nails it is advisable to wrap a piece of soft leather or a piece of fabric round the hammer head, as this stops the nails from being bruised.

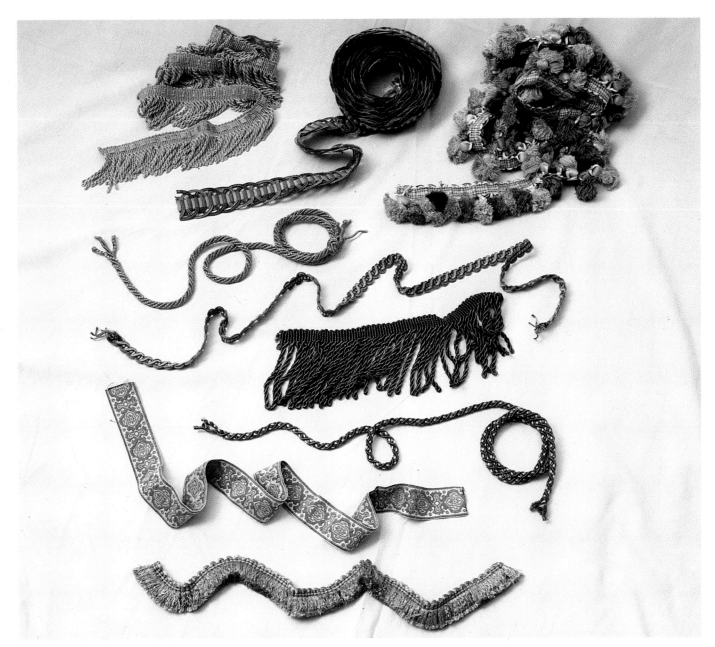

A selection of gimps and braids

USEFUL ADDRESSES

The Association of Master Upholsterers
348 Neasden Lane
London NW1 U 0EP
01–205 0465

Beckfoot Mill Ltd (filling materials)
Howden Road
Silsden, near Keighley
West Yorkshire
0535 53358

Surrey Trimmings Ltd (upholstery sundries)
16 St Dunstans Hill
Sutton
Surrey
01–644 9201

Pilgrim Payne and Co Ltd (specialist cleaners)
Park Street Works
Latimer Place
London W10 6QA

Distinctive Trimmings (trimmings, fringes)
17 Kensington Church Street
London W8 4LF
01–937 6174

D L Forester Ltd
(DIY upholstery sundries, mail order service)
12 The Ongar Trading Estate
20 Ongar Road
Great Dunmow
Essex CM6 1EU
0371 5201

GLOSSARY

Accommodate	make room for
Back tack	tack invisibly
Back tack strip	length of plastic or metal used to make a smooth edge
Back up	to fill in a section and reinforce the fabric
Bridle stitch	stitch sewn into hessian to hold stuffing in place
Buckram	hessian impregnated with glue to form a stiff cloth
Buttoning	application of buttons through fabric to hold pleats or to decorate
Clean out	to make smooth by pulling the fabric to remove puckering
Close nail	decorative nails placed together to form a continuous line
Collar	extra piece of fabric joined to a curve to make a smooth tuck in
Cut sheet	cutting and estimating plan
Ease in	work fabric into a smaller area
Facing	covered shape, used to tidy or decorate front or back scrolls
First stuffing	first stage of stuffing
Flush	level with
Flys	piece of fabric sewn on to make extra length in tuck-in area
Gimp	a narrow braid
Gimping	applying gimp trimming
Girt	a tight line across the fabric caused by packing stuffing down too hard
Lip	front edge of seat joined to platform
Marking up	marking fabric with chalk or marker
Mitre	folding a corner to make fabric lie flat
Notch	V-shaped cut in seam allowance
Piping used as trimming	crossway strips with cord inserted
Platform cloth	cloth used instead of main fabric usually on the seat
Proud	in front of
Purchase	obtain maximum power
Scroll	a curved shape usually on chair front (see facing)
Second stuffing	after the stitched edge comes the second stuffing.
Shy	just short of (opposite of proud)
Skewer	a long type of pin which holds fabric in place
Slipping thread	fine lining thread used for slip stitching
Sound	in good order
Stuffing ties	ties of twine sewn right through stuffing to hold it in place
Swell	protruding layer of stuffing

Tack home..tack right into the frame
Tack line..line of tacks in the frame
Take-up..extra fabric used when quilting or fluting
Temporary tack.....................................tack only halfway just to hold the fabric
Tie off..knot ends to secure
Top cover..finishing fabric
To the thread.......................................to the line of the thread across the weft of the fabric
To trim..apply trimming
Trim..cut fabric back to seam line
Tuck-in..areas between seat back and inside arm, where fabric tucks out of sight
Up to calico...ready for top cover
'W' formation.......................................tacks placed to form a 'W' shape
Welt..used as a trimming on leather or fabric (see piping)

INDEX

Page numbers in *italics* refer to illustrations.

arms
    independent sprung 31–3, *32, 33*
    re-covering 52–5, *53, 56*

back, independent sprung 33–4
'backing up' 31, *32*
blind stitching 22, *23*, 42
border-edged headboard *see* headboards
braiding 73, *75*
bridle stitching 11, *11*, 20
buttoning 66, 71
    see also float buttoning

calico, fitting of
    drop in seat 12, *12*
    independent sprung edge 31
    overstuff seat 24–5
close nailing 74
cording 73
covering and re-covering 44–74
cushion pads, making of
    bordered *61, 62*, 62–3, *63, 64*
    flat 60–2
    gathered corner 63–4, *65*
'cut sheet' 45

deep-button-backed chair *see* iron-frame chair
deep-button-backed headboard *see* headboards
dining seat
    drop in 9–13, *12*
    overstuff 15–25, *16, 18, 24, 25*

easy chair, sprung
    re-covering *47, 48, 50*, 50–8, *51, 52, 53, 54, 55, 56, 57*
    re-seating 26–34

edge stitching, 23–4, *24*
equipment 7–9

fabrics, covering
    estimating amounts 45, 47, 65
    types of 44
facings 37
float buttoning 67, *68*
fluting 57–8, *58, 59*
flys 45, 50, *55*
fringe *73*

gimp 73, *75*

half-hitch knot 18–19, *19*
headboards
    border-edged 67–9, *68, 69, 71*
    deep-button-backed 37–9, 65–7, *66*
hessian
    drop in seat 11, *11*
    iron-frame chair 40, *41, 42*
hitch knot 18–19, *19*

independent sprung arm, 31–3, *32, 33*
independent sprung back 33–4
independent sprung edge *28*, 28–31, *29, 30*
iron-frame chair
    re-covering *44*, 70–3, *71, 72*
    ripping out 39
    upholstering 39–42, *40, 43*

knots 16, *16*, 18–19, *19*

laid cord 17–18, *18*

lashing (lacing) of springs
    independent sprung edge 29
    overstuff seat 17–19, *18, 19*
locking knot *19*
loose seats 13–15

materials 8–9
measurements, taking of 45, 47

overstuff dining chair 15–25, *16, 18, 24, 25*

paper pattern 45
pin cushion seat 15
piping (welting) 47–50, *49, 50*
platform seat, covering of 51

re-covering 44–74
regulator, use of 22
ripping out 9, *9*, 39
ruching 50

scrim, fitting of
    independent sprung edge 30–1
    iron-frame chair 40–1, *41, 42*
    overstuff seat 20–1, *21*
scrolls 55–7, *57*
slip knot 16, *16*
spoon back chair 41
spring canvas, fitting of 19–20, *20*
springs
    sewing in *16*, 16–17
    lashing 17–19, *18, 19*, 29
    independent sprung arm 31–2
    independent sprung back 34
    independent sprung edge 28–9, *29, 30*

stools 13–15
stuffing 11–12, *20*, 20–1, 28

tack roll method 13–14, *14*
tarpaulin, fitting of 19–20, *20*
tools 7, *7*

trimmings and finishes 73–4, *75*
tuck-in 45

van dykeing 65–6, *66, 67*

wadding, positioning of 12–13

webbing 10, *10, 11*
welting (piping) 47–50, *49, 50*
wings
   re-covering *59*, 59–60, *61*
   upholstering 36, *36*